—PRAISES FOR *Always Wear Lipstick*

"We smile through our tears as Karen Winston allows us to journey into her most intimate moments. Her touching wit and charming yet searing writing, affords us a poignant picture of this author's soul..."

Janis Forgotson
popular artist, teacher and scholar

"This book looks with quiet poignancy into the silent insecurity of religious persecution, childhood inhibitions, racism and other topics. Winston's melodic voice on the page is paired with discovery as she ambles through vignettes of her 1950's childhood. Quoting her mother in a short essay on weight, she writes, "Being ashamed is such a sad way to be. Isn't it?"

Lauren Camp
poet, teacher author of Dorset prize-winning,
One Hundred Hungers

"This collection of short vignettes reflects the historical social and political landscape of Washington DC, 1950's, as well the upheavals that occurred during the l960s. The book gives us visual snapshots into the life of a Jewish girl facing obstacles of self-esteem. Accurately portrayed and well written."

Margaret Bartley
author of award winning biography, *GRISHA*

"*Karen's Always Wear Lipstick And Other Myths My Mother Told Me captures another time, another era. It's in the details. Karen's unique voice brings lightness and humor to dark situations. Her personal story combined with her astute observations of people around her make this a riveting read.*"

Hadiyah Carlyle

author, *Torch in the Dark: One Woman's Journey*

"*Karen Winston's essays reveal her talent to write about her life with humor and pathos. Documenting a mother's advice to please others, she overcame conflicts of self-deprecation with sould desrching philosophy and dedication to expressing herself in writing. We have worked together for years to birth ALWAYS WEAR LIPSTICK and today I am proud to say her baby has arrived*".

Ronni Miller

Book Midwife/Developmental Editor author of *Dance With The Elephants: Free Your Creativity and Write*, *Cocoon to Butterfly: A Metamorphosis of Personal Growth Through Expressive Writing and Domestic Shorts*

"*The trauma of women in the 1950's and 1960's will never be over and is brought to life in this subtle and incisive memoir. The author's acute observations of the beauty preparations of women during that era is enough to make any woman shudder.*"

Pat Murphy

author of *Searching for Spring* and *We Walk The Back of the Tiger*

Always Wear Lipstick

BY

KAREN WINSTON

Illustration art by Jill Pankey

the *Peppertree Press*

Sarasota, Florida

This is a work of Creative Nonfiction,
as are all recollected events, draped in memories,
colored by time and passion.

Cover and interior illustrations by Jill Pankey's Lipstick Series

For information regarding permission,
call 941-922-2662 or contact us at our website:
www.peppertreepublishing.com or write to:
the Peppertree Press, LLC.
Attention: Publisher
1269 First Street, Suite 7
Sarasota, Florida 34236

ISBN: 978-1-61493-590-2

Library of Congress Number: 2018906651

Printed March 2019

Acknowledgements

I am forever grateful to Julie Fretzin, my editor, my voice on the phone, to extraordinary artist Jill Pankey, my "sista", and to Sara Eyestone, brilliant director of all things art. To La Posada Hotel in Santa Fe, New Mexico, for the Thursday morning hospitality, and the unlimited hot chocolate. To the gathering of our writers, warmed by the blazing fire in the bar and creative spirits stalking these historic grounds. And of course, to my Hubby. Much love.

Contents

THE STARS ARE THERE — 137

art by Jill Pank

GROWING UP IN THE FIFTIES

Washington, D.C., 1955

I was a child of our nation's capital. When I was young, I would shop with my mother on F Street in Washington, D.C. It was a time of pale-green trolley cars and grand shopping at Garfinkel's Department Store.

I would enter the first floor, where the sensuous aroma of white gardenias filtered the rarefied air. Women in hats and heels would walk directly to the white glove department and be waited on immediately.

"May I help you?" the pleasant voice would inquire.

There was never a moment's wait or a request too big or too small.

"Here, let me help you button the wrist of that glove."

White women would shop for white gloves and veiled hats.

"Girdles and lingerie, third floor," called the elevator operator, dressed with his red and gold jacket with fringed epaulets.

"Clang," and a hand on the handle would pull open the elevator cage door for the well-heeled women and perhaps, as in our case, their young daughters. At the end of lingerie was the delightful teashop where we would order lunch with the older, white haired women. A waitress in a pale blue waist dress with a ruffled white collar and a crisply ironed apron would descend from nowhere. She would appear like a swift sparrow sailing in from the open sky.

"Tea?" she would ask. Always Lipton. No Earl Gray or English Breakfast in those days. She would deliver a tray of whipped cream

3

delights, and I would listen to the sounds of Lawrence Welk or Perry Como drip from the fingers of the piano player in the far right corner. The notes would float above the steam of steeped tea and the sugar would descend to the table dripping in the sunlit dust.

Always Wear Lipstick

I pull on my shorts, which are too tight. I wrap my bathing suit into my pink towel, grab the bundle, and rush to the hot pavement outside my home.

My mother and I are headed to Indian Springs Country Club, an enclave of middle class America, mostly Jewish, in suburban Maryland. It is a hot summer morning, and I have a swimming lesson with Bill.

My mother will sit with her friends on a hot chaise lounge. When she gets up for a dip, during "adult swim," the pool will be empty of kids splashing and yelling. She will don her tight white bathing cap and snap the strap under her chin.

Clutching tightly to my towel and bathing suit, I skip down our front steps to the waiting car. I picture the chlorine pool and my best friend, who will be waiting. We'll gobble hot dogs and hamburgers and slurp vanilla milkshakes. We'll play "Go Fish" with the moldy cards they stash under the bushes near the ladies' locker room. We'll do headstands in the water while our shriveled fingers support us from the bottom of the pool.

Opening the passenger door, I feel the hot air hit me like flames. The interior is black. July is blazing with intense summer heat. It hurts my fingers to touch the door handle; rolling down the passenger window, I wait on the sticky seat.

My mother emerges from the front door, a wide belt around her waist and a black and white patterned skirt, short enough to

5

display her trim ankles and her shiny high heels. The hot air blows through the car as the driver's door swings open.

"Where is your lipstick?" she asks me.

I pull down the car visor and peer at my chubby face in the mirror. My hair is parted on the right side with a barrette. I look at the freckles on the bridge of my nose.

My mother glares, disappointed in my plain face and my round tummy. I see it in her eyes. My heart is a small sponge, and I know I'm not enough. Never enough.

Not Everyone Welcome

"Hi ho, hi ho, it's off to Glen Echo!"

Four little voices ring at the top of their five-year old lungs. We are piled into the back of my mother's car—me and my brother Mike, my best friend Stephanie, and Jim, the boy who lives across the street.

Today is a special day; we have been waiting forever for this event.

"You all ready?" asks Wilma, our live-in maid. Her black skin shines against her white, freshly pressed uniform, her teeth glowing in a bright smile. She is as excited as the kids. Glen Echo is the local amusement park. The "dodge-em" cars, the carousel, the huge roller coaster that she is still afraid of—magic waiting for her.

It is a long ride to Glen Echo in the summer heat. The windows are wide open; the breeze blows my friend's hair into her mouth. She spits it out as we sing our song and clap our hands.

After what seems like forever, we arrive at the magical amusement park. We hear the shrieks of fear and the loud laughter. I smell the popcorn and the hot dogs and the chlorine from the largest swimming pool in the D.C. area. It's too early for the lights to be on, and the temperature is sweltering. We don't care. This is the day. The one extraordinary day that summer of 1954 when we can go on all the rides we want. Our stomachs will tumble and thrill.

"OK, kids," says my mother. "Stay with Wilma. I will be back at four o'clock."

My mother walks us to the gate. There are three ticket takers at the window. My mother buys the tickets. Then we hear the conversation. We don't understand what is happening. The voices are hushed. My mother heads back to the hot car.

"Wilma can't go in."

"But why?" I ask, holding Wilma's hand and struggling to see the top of the roller coaster.

"Because. . . ." My mother never tells me why. We leave the park. The air is stifling. We get ice cream. This is no consolation for us.

Later, Glen Echo closes when the Civil Rights Acts of the '60s force the owners to integrate their park and their pristine chlorine pool.

"Valid any day of the week, except Sundays and Holidays," shouted the black script on the front of the small green 1954 tickets.

Not everyone was welcome.

Puppy

a little puppy, too small to wear a collar, snuggled next to me in front of the TV in the living room. I watched Mickey Mouse and Annette while the little bundle of fur sat beside me on the sofa. I had always dreamed of my own puppy, and yesterday my dad brought one home to me. I cuddled the little guy and smelled his sweet puppy breath.

"Be careful with him," my dad warned. He handed me the silky puppy with deep brown eyes.

"Get that dog off of the furniture," my mother yelled from the kitchen. "Take him outside."

I carried the dog out of the house to visit my neighborhood friends. I pulled my red wagon out from under the porch, blew the dust and dirt from the corners, and placed the little puppy in the middle.

"Lassie," I said, naming him after another of my favorite TV shows.

I softly placed the baby dog on the hard lacquered surface and took off.

I pulled the puppy up Navaho Drive to visit my best friend, Debby. Debby took one look at the limpid brown eyes on the tiny animal and grabbed him.

"Oh. . . oh. . . he is so soft," said my friend and squeezed Lassie between her five-year-old palms. Hugs and kisses followed and then another very tight squeeze.

"Bye-bye, Baby," said Debby, and I wheeled my little puppy to visit my other neighbor, Doreen.

I traveled down Twelfth Avenue, a very steep hill, and little Lassie slipped back and forth in the wagon. I wiped the white foam from his mouth and patted his head.

Twelve neighborhood pals kicked the dodge ball in Doreen's front yard. Bruce was first to catch a glimpse of the puppy. He sprang over to the little red wagon and grabbed the tiny puppy.

"Catch!" he said to his friend and tossed Lassie as if he were a rubber ball.

"Stop it!" I cried when I saw the little dog fall on the grass. "Give me back my baby!"

Doreen came over, squeezed Lassie affectionately, and then she waved good-bye after kissing the puppy over and over on his face. She may have held the neck a bit too tight.

I placed my puppy back in the middle of the wagon and, in the Indian summer heat, I took him down the steep hill to the corner of Twelfth Avenue and Chickasaw Drive. Lassie rolled back and forth in the wagon, and his body hit the sides once or twice. He never fell out.

Now the puppy's breathing was heavy, the panting sounded loud, and his little pink tongue hung out of the right side of his mouth.

I dragged the wagon up the ten steps to my front door. Bumbity-bump. . . bumbity-bump and I, along with the puppy, was at the top of the concrete steps.

Wilma, our maid, was first to see me and Lassie at the front door. "What did you do to this puppy?" she asked. "Your Mama and Papa shoulda' never let you take that dog alone. You are too little. I don't know what they were thinking!"

I reached for my puppy and placed him in the cardboard box with a pillow. I sat by that box for hours waiting for him to move, to lick my hand the way he did just hours before.

Nothing. Lassie never moved again. I touched the lifeless body.

"Will he be OK?" I cried, the puppy's body now stiff and cold.

I sat by that box until the body was stone. Then I cried big wet tears. I felt something in my stomach, a sharp pain, that I had never felt before. It hurt.

I stroked the fur on the still, cold bundle of soft puppy in the corner of that cardboard box. I sat for a long time and waited for my mother to come home.

Soon Wilma called me for dinner, and the sun went down behind the fence. "There's nothing we can do," said Wilma as she tucked me into my bed, stroked my forehead, and kissed my cheek. "Your mama will be back soon," said Wilma, and I drifted off to sleep under the warmth of my soft blankets.

Playdate

I was six, and she was six, and we shared our first grade class-room. Langley Park Elementary School serviced the bed-room communities of Silver Spring, Maryland, just outside of Washington, D.C. The elementary schools were bloated with post-war baby boomers, looking to start a life on the freshly paved asphalt streets with newly planted grasses. Segregation was ram-pant. We had colored bathrooms and separate schools. Our old textbooks went to Booker Elementary in neighborhoods closer to D.C.

On the first day of school, I was seated next to Bobbie Jones. She was a blonde, blue-eyed Christian. We both loved jump rope and dodge ball, so we became fast friends on the playground dur-ing recess.

"Come over and play after school," she said.

I told my mother that night that I had met a best friend. Her name was Bobbie, and we played jacks and read comic books. She had lots of Archie and Veronica.

The next morning, I rode the yellow bus to school. I knew I wouldn't be returning home on that bus because I was going home with Bobbie, my new best friend. All day we giggled and anticipated the fun we would have on our first playdate.

After the very long school day, the afternoon bell rang, and we lined up for her school bus, which was #33, not #241 like mine. We sat in the back of the bus with our other friends, and soon the bus rolled onto her street. She lived on Navajo, and I lived on Chickasaw. Our neighborhood community was Indian Spring.

We jumped off of the bus and rushed to her front door.

"Mom! Mom?" Bobbie called. When there was no answer, she said, "I guess my mom is next door visiting her friend. Let's play in my bedroom." We were clutching her Tiny Tears dolls when the front door opened. Bobbie's mother walked into the kitchen.

"Bobbie? Bobbie? Are you here?"

"Yes, Mom," Bobbie answered. Then she said to me, "I have to go tell my mother we're playing. Hide under here." I scrambled under the bed beneath her mattress, hidden by her dust ruffles.

I heard Bobbie and her mom in the kitchen. "We have to call her mother to pick her up."

"But why, Mommy?"

I hear the words but have trouble understanding. "Don't you know her name is Karen Weinstein?" Bobbie's mother's voice rang in my ears, which were as alert as a cat's listening for strange noises. "Weinstein. Weinstein."

I was told to call my mother. I picked up the kitchen phone with the snake-like cord.

Ring. . . Ring. But my mother didn't answer. She knew I was playing with Bobbie.

Bobbie's mom told us to get in the car.

"She forgot to offer cookies or milk," I thought. She asked me to sit in the back seat, and we were shuttled to my front door, where she dropped me off at the curb. I sat on the front steps as I watched her green car drive away, taking with it my best friend Bobbie and all hopes of winning at jacks.

Wilma's Room

My mother wasn't there. There was silence in my home. My mother was working or lunching or shopping. She was playing cards or sleeping. The maid was there. Not my mother. It was Wilma who lived in the basement in a tiny room built into our 1950s semi-detached home. The maid's room was clean and new when we first lived on Chickasaw Drive. Over the years, it took a character of its own. Dungeon-like. The floors carpeted in dingy moss green, the walls beige. Colorless. The maid's room was in the same area as the laundry, dark with no windows. A faint smell of Clorox and mold permeated the air.

There was a twin bed, a dresser and a lamp. The bulb was dim under a faded shade. I would only go into that room when Wilma wasn't there. When it was silent. There were no pictures of her family on the dresser. No forgotten rings or bracelets in a tray. No half-open bottles of cheap perfume.

I can't remember visiting her in that silent space. It was suffocating. One Thanksgiving, my cousins and my brother Mike, who was five at the time, played school. We took over her room so the adults would be far away. The walls were knotty pine, and the room smelled like Wilma, who may have been using her pomade to style her short black hair. There was a small closet. In that closet was a yellow uniform and an apron. Clothing hanging like a spider's web in the corner of a window that hadn't been opened in months.

Wilma left us sometime during my childhood. Before I was ten and the family moved from that home to a larger space without a Wilma's room. I don't remember a farewell. I remember the room, emptied and silent until another maid would come to fill that space and linger for a year or two.

Teachers

In that little room in the back of the knotty pine basement, I am the teacher. Iris and Lynn, my cousins, are my students. This is my classroom.

We have finished Thanksgiving dinner, and the grown-ups are upstairs talking. I have a blackboard and white chalk.

"4+4=8," I instruct my students as I scribble numbers on the chalkboard resting on an oak stand. "Be quiet, boys and girls," I admonish.

We have allowed my little brother Mike to enter the room. He had been pounding on the door for an hour. "Mike," I say, "Sit down and be quiet!"

Mike sits with his five-year-old legs hanging over the end of the little blue chair in the tiny room. This is the maid's room when it is not our classroom. The maid is off tonight. It is a holiday, and she must have a family somewhere with kids and cousins and such. But, to me, that is not a reality. Wilma lives in our home and only in our home. I can't imagine her anywhere else.

"Who wants to be the teacher now?" I ask my motley class.

"My turn," answers Iris, and she stands in front of the room with her skirt caught between her skinny legs. She picks up the white chalk. I sit in her seat.

"Now," she orders, "We will sing this song. . . All together now, one, two, three. How much is that doggie in the window? The one with the waggly tail?"

Mike, with soulful eyes and a big voice chants, "How much is that doggie in the window?"

Soon, we are raucous. We love this song and chant it over and over, clapping our hands with the beat that cousin Iris taps with the pencil on the edge of the blackboard. "How much is that doggie in the window? I DO hope that doggie's for sale!"

Pirate Bill and the Contest

"You won the contest!" my mother announces.

"What contest?" I ask.

"Wilma answered the phone this afternoon. Pirate Bill called. He said that you won the award and that you will be on TV for the Halloween Show."

"I will?" I ask.

I had written to Pirate Bill and told him what I liked best about his show. The TV program, which aired at 4:00, before Howdy Doody but after Mickey Mouse, showed Bullwinkle cartoons. I wrote about how much I loved Bullwinkle and Friends. I asked Wilma to mail the letter for me.

My mother says, "We'll have Audrey, the seamstress, make a costume for you. You'll be a gypsy!" Audrey wraps a flowing scarf around my light brown hair and pulls a swirling skirt around my waist. Last is the silk blouse with puffy sleeves. My mother places jewelry that feels cold and heavy around my neck.

At the TV studio, I am decked in gypsy folds. Another boy is dressed as a bolt of lightning. He has four cardboard boxes stacked on his body and all are wrapped in aluminum foil.

A bicycle is the first prize in the costume contest. It has a bar across the top, but I hope that, if I win the first prize, I will get a girl's bike. Maybe a pink one with a basket on the handlebars.

Then comes the parade, and all the children walk around in a circle past the judges. My scarves fly like a kite. My long gypsy skirt sweeps the floor of the wooden studio, blowing the dust and rearranging the wires that slither around the corners like snakes in a pit.

Pirate Bill announces, "Kids, line up here. Time for the prizes!"

I look at that red bicycle with envy. I know that some boy will win and that it will be "lightning." I win third prize for my gypsy costume. Lightning wins first.

Third prize is a collection of Charles Dickens' works, bound in dark blue and trimmed in gold. The books follow us home and are placed on the shelf next to the World Book Encyclopedias. They aren't fun to read. Not like Nancy Drew or Double Date. I hope that some day my mom and dad will buy me a pink bike without a bar. I don't care what happens to those dusty old books.

A Grim Fairy Tale

At school Mrs. Darwin weighs me on the scale in the front of the classroom. "140 pounds," she announces and writes the fat number next to my name in the grade book.

Pretty soon I will go to Junior High, and I will be fat there, too. I'm always at the end of the line because my last name is at the end of the alphabet. Fat and last. Last to be picked for dodge ball on the playground. Last to have a date to the sixth grade prom. Finally, Peter asks me to be his date. We're good friends. He is picked last, too.

My mother takes me shopping for a new dress for the prom. The salesgirl brings in different dresses, beginning at size 12, which won't zip, to a 14, which almost zips, and I find I am 16. The dress is blue with a white sailor collar and a red bow at the neck. I don't love the dress, but, at least it fits, and I can go home. We'll head to my grandmother's house and have the dress hemmed and fitted.

My grandmother will ask her customers to wait in her small apartment while she adjusts the needle and the thread, the straight pins in her mouth, and the thimble she wears on her gnarled finger. Even when she watches Perry Como or Lawrence Welk, she is sewing and wearing the thimble.

Later that evening, I'm reading in bed and wishing I was a twin with a thin body, long dark hair and a boyfriend like the girls in the book, Double Date.

My mother begins her nighttime story. "When I was a little girl," she tells me, "I had a big, big nose. I lived in Scranton, Pennsylvania, and everyone at Central High School was Catholic."

"The Catholics would call me 'Jew' or 'Murderer of Christ.' They called me a 'Yid' or a 'Kike.' They called me 'Big nose' and worse. Your grandmother would sew all of my clothes, none of them had any style at all. Not like the pretty dress I bought for you today. Grandma could hardly speak English. And your grandfather, he was a peddler from Poland. He carried a black satchel on his back and wandered up and down the hills of town selling needles and thread. I was ashamed when I was a little girl. Being ashamed is such a sad way to be, isn't it?"

Then my mother kisses me goodnight and tiptoes away, out the closed door and into the dark hall.

Silence

It was hot that Saturday afternoon. My mother dropped me off, as usual, at the matinee at the Allen Movie Theatre. I hated The Three Musketeers. I didn't like the men with long curly black hair, sombrero hats, and long sharp swords. I wanted to go home. As I left the dark of the theater, the sunlight made me blink. I expected a long walk home, but I had no idea how long a walk it would be.

Wiping my brow, I thought, "I need water. I'm thirsty." After what seemed like miles and miles, I stopped at a corner of Sligo Creek Parkway where the woods left shadows on the hot pavement. I stood on the shady corner, lost and tired, a perfect target for one who was hunting.

My mother never told me about taking rides with strangers. No need to warn children in the middle 1950s. There were no child predators then. It was safe to go to the movies on a Saturday. It was safe to drop off your little girl with her friends and know that she would come right home after the popcorn and after the magic show at intermission. The magician had a moustache. He had a tall black hat and a bunny.

I wanted to go home where it was cool. I accepted the ride with the man who looked like the magician with the black moustache. I sat on the other side of the front seat—no seatbelts then. No consoles in the middle.

"Sit next to me," he said. "My little girl lets me put my fingers in her like this."

I started to cry and stare out of the window. I gazed at the familiar Eagle's Five and Dime where I bought trading cards to barter with friends during summer afternoons. I saw Lansburg's Department Store, where my mother bought my clothes and where I was in a hula-hoop contest. I was sobbing because the man was touching me.

I recognized my grandmother's corner brick apartment when the man with the moustache asked, "Is this where you live?"

"I live near here," I stuttered, my sweat twisted with tears like mixed shiny beads. "I live around that corner." I pointed to my house.

"Get out and walk home."

I got out of the car and walked, each step a trial.

"Mommy, Mommy," I choked out the scary story.

"Shhhhhh," my mother said. "Don't tell anyone."

That was the end of the story. We never talked about it again.

I did tell my best friend Debby the secret, but for absolution, I added that my mother scrubbed me with alcohol and gave me a bath. I wanted to be cared for. I wanted to be clean again.

"Shhhh, don't tell anyone." And I kept silent just as my mother instructed.

I Have A Dream

I took the green and white bus from my safe Maryland neighborhood, pulled out my thirty-five cents, and headed to the dangerous regions of downtown Washington, D.C. I lived with my mother, my much-detested stepfather, stepsister, stepbrother and my very own brother, just a year younger than me. Two families had blended into one just months earlier, moving into this suburban split-level that looked like every other home in the neighborhood built in 1962.

817 Venice Drive sat next to empty fields, cows, and muddy construction sites. The neighborhood could not grow any faster. Homes sprouted like dollar weeds on a green playing field, one after the other. The families moved in with their children, many of whom were my classmates. Springbrook High, that was the name of my new school, and I was in the ninth grade, along with my stepsister, who was only six months younger.

So, on this sunny day in August, for no apparent reason that I can remember, I was alone on the bus heading to a march that I had read about in the Washington Post. Martin Luther King was going to speak at the mall, and everyone was buzzing about this huge "march thing." I was only fifteen. Too young to drive, no friends interested enough to spend a Saturday on a political cause, I decided to go it alone.

Somewhere in the deep recesses of my brain or my heart, I felt magnetized to the event. Maybe it was the turmoil in my own family, the separation I felt at the loss of my father, the integration of my new step-family, the need to understand this blending of cultures. Who knew? All I was aware of on that day in 1962 was the oppressive heat, the brilliant sun, and the humming of the wheels on the big bus that drove down New Hampshire Avenue to the crowded Washington Mall.

I was shocked to see a white woman holding the hand of a black man. I tried not to stare, but I had never seen that before in my pristine white neighborhood in suburban Maryland. Some marcher pasted a big button on my sleeveless shirt. "I am a civil rights marcher," the button screamed in red letters. Then, I was carrying a cardboard placard on a wooden stick. "We Shall Overcome" were the printed words on the sign in my hands, and soon I was swept away by the moving crowd, the numbers unimaginable, this huge mass of humanity, black and white, man, woman and child, pressed against one another.

Sweat poured from the brow of the black person in front of me, and I felt the moist tear-stained cheek of the woman next to me. Together we marched, step by step, one foot in front of the other, until we reached the mall where Martin Luther King readied to make his speech. "I Have a Dream," he declared, surrounded by Ralph Abernathy, body guards, and a sea of worshipping followers.

King's words sent chills down my spine. I was too young to understand much of it. But goose bumps appeared as, from my heart, a stirring began inside me as I listened deeply to the melodic words, sung softy in reverence, of "We shall overcome some daaaaay."

A spirit descended upon the crowd like a blanket of possibility. I felt it in my veins, the change in the air. This was a new feeling, and I couldn't quite separate the rushing beating noises of the crowd from my own pulse hammering inside my head under the hot sun that sweltering August day.

Somewhere, without a doubt, lines would be blurred, and like my new family that I struggled to comprehend, the world would change. Black and white would merge, and that was fine with me.

That day I didn't know about the violence to follow. I didn't know about the flames that would rage just blocks from where I was standing that day, clutching my cardboard placard, wearing my aluminum button. I didn't know about bullets that would be shot from balconies by unlikely and suspicious persons. How could I? My tender aged skin, sunburned and flushed with excitement, felt the blanket of hope today. I didn't know how it would melt like a raspberry creamsicle held by a ten-year-old, slippery stains left like blood mixed with bleach on a crisp white tee shirt.

I could have shopped at Jelleff's with my friends, bought popcorn at the movies and held hands with Robbie, my most recent boyfriend. I could have stayed home and watched the march on the TV in our newly carpeted plush family room. But that morning, that sunny day in August, I left my own home where my mother was the "new mother" to a new brother and a new sister. A family created out of unlikely rag-tag orphans, where the "old mother" of the house had died of brain cancer just a year earlier. My mother became the "new mother," dressed in polyester and wrapped in red lipstick.

Loose Powder

*M*y grandmother, Frieda Benjamin, used loose face powder. Not the kind in a compact but the kind that was soft and would cake on her face and deepen her wrinkles. When I was three or four, my grandmother would send hand-sewn clothing for my doll. I would sit on the cold cement sidewalk in front of my little home surrounded by a chain link fence and tear open that box from Scranton, Pennsylvania.

After my grandfather died, my grandmother moved from Scranton, Pennsylvania to Maryland. She was a peddler's wife from Lithuania. She would tell me of her shtetel in the old country. My grandmother spoke many languages—Russian, Polish, Yiddish, Lithuanian, German, English.

She was bent over and wore a babushka on her head as she walked to the grocery store pulling her wire basket on wheels. Her fingers were crooked and bent from sewing with the thread my grandfather, Sam, left when he died. That was all he left. No money—just black and white thread on wooden spools. My grandmother would repair clothing for neighborhood women, letting out the waists of skirts, shortening the hems of coats or replacing lost buttons. She always placed a silver thimble on her middle finger.

At lunch, I would walk to her apartment from my first grade classroom. It was a long walk up that hill to get to her kitchen to eat Velveeta cheese, sandwiched between tuna fish and white bread.

One day, while I was visiting my grandmother, I saw my Aunt

Irene and Uncle Bob, my mother's brother, who had just arrived from Philadelphia. Aunt Irene told me that she always wanted a little girl as she was the mother of two boys, my male cousins, Ivan and Bobby. She was rich and beautiful, and so different from my Grandmother Freida. Every Christmas, Aunt Irene would send my family small black and white photos with white scalloped edges. The photos showed the Benjamins celebrating Christmas, decorating the tree like my Christian neighbors. Their life seemed so golden.

One day, my cousin Bobby found his father swinging from the ceiling beam in the front office of their Philadelphia furniture store. Bobby had to climb a ladder to cut the rope, then call my Aunt Irene and ask her to drive to their place of business and help him. The terrible information came from Aunt Irene late in the afternoon on a Friday in early fall. My mother ran to Grandma's kitchen to shout the horrible news. Grandma Benjamin was making potato latkes as was her usual habit on the Sabbath. A large bowl filled with shredded potatoes rested on her counter. She ignored my mother and continued to stir the thick mixture. It was as if she were deaf and couldn't hear the words. Finally, she acknowledged her son had died. She quietly put her pots and pans away and slipped into her bedroom to be alone.

A few days later, the family traveled to Philadelphia for Uncle Bob's funeral. Aunt Irene's friends wore beautiful clothing and had Vidal Sassoon styled hair, cut sharply on an angle across the cheek. The women had black hair and gobs of black eyeliner defining their heavily mascaraed eyelashes. Everything seemed black and white and shiny. My grandmother stood in the corner with that fringed black babushka tied under her chin.

She had brushed her hair and tucked it into a bun with the help of a soft wire donut tied with large wire bobby pins. I don't remember seeing my grandmother cry. I remember her silver hair. It was so long and silky. And her face was coated with fresh powder.

Grandfather

Soon after my Grandfather Benjamin died, my mother began to tell me about him. It's as if she were a corked bottle of champagne, waiting for a vintage year before exploding.

"Your Grandfather was a Communist. I remember that he went to a meeting every night when I was a little girl. I would sit at the window in Grandma's living room that overlooked Main Street and watch him leave."

I began to imagine his black coat trailing in the evening breeze, his head bundled in a wool cap as the snow piled up on the street. In my mind, it was always snowing in Scranton, Pennsylvania.

"But what IS a Communist?" I demanded. I watched my father sitting on the lounge chair in front of our TV, and in between turning the crinkly pages of the Washington Post, he would listen to a man he said was named "McCarthy." This man hated Communists. My father was sure of this.

I knew that the Communists were going to drop a bomb on my third grade classroom.

I sat in the third row, center desk. Once a week, I became the "bomb captain," and it was my job to make sure the class would "Duck and Cover." When the "WOO WOO" of an eerie siren screamed through the playground and tore into the chalky dust of Mrs. Freeman's room, I called out "Duck and Cover!"

Everyone would then scramble under wooden desks. Our

hearts would beat, fear would flow, and we would wait for the bomb. I would cover my head with my hands, fold into a fetal position, and wait. Then the catastrophe would be over when the siren sounded. The class would return to spelling. Just like that. . . bomb, and then spell.

I thought, "My grandfather was a Communist," but he was dead and no longer could drop the bombs. I guessed that was a good thing.

Jealousy

"Aunt Reva is so beautiful," I think as I admire my aunt's tiny body and her trim, tan legs emerging from her red convertible. She's wearing a halter-top and white shorts. I think she looks like Elizabeth Taylor, and I love Elizabeth Taylor.

My mother looks so different. She's tall with lacquered blonde hair and watery blue eyes. My mother seems sad. I never know why, but think it must be my fault.

"Hi, Sweetie!" Aunt Reva calls from the hot sidewalk. She kisses me on the cheek, leaving a smear from her lipstick. She gently wipes it off of my cheek.

"Where's Mom?" she asks.

"Getting dressed." My mother takes a long time to get dressed when she has lunch with my aunt. My mother checks her lipstick, her skirt, and her eye make-up. When she comes to the front door, she has eye shadow deeply matted, and it slips into the creases on her eyelids.

I think my mother doesn't like Aunt Reva very much. She says mean things about her. She says that Aunt Reva steals her friends and makes them her own. Does Aunt Reva say bad things behind my mother's back like my mother tells me? Selfish, that's what my mother says. . . Aunt Reva is selfish. I'm confused because I adore my aunt. She is the mother of my favorite cousins, Lynn and Iris. But today my mother and my aunt act like they are best friends.

That night, I hear my mother whispering on the telephone.

She has covered the mouthpiece with her manicured hand, and I want to know what she is saying. I tiptoe to the bedroom and pick up the receiver.

"Janice," my mother is saying to her closest friend, "I followed Reva the other day when she got her hair done." Joe's Buick was there. Right where you said it would be. He was waiting for her. Reva was wearing one of those sexy outfits and short shorts. Joe hugged her and then climbed into her car. I don't know where they went."

I hang up the phone and tip-toe to my bedroom to read Nancy Drew. I pull the book from under the pillow. I feel sad that my mother and Janice don't like Aunt Reva. I know where Joe and Reva went. Lisa, my friend, is Joe's daughter. He bought her a Tiny Tears doll last week. The kind of doll that cries real tears and wets her diapers.

Lisa and I play SPUD all summer in the evening when the crickets croak and the misty humid dusk fades to dark. I ask Lisa, "Don't you love your doll?"

Joe, Lisa's father, would never know which doll to buy. Aunt Reva was the one who helped him. She is good at surprises. Fathers never know about dolls and stuff.

The Chair

*L*ight shadows the face. The chair sits in the corner of the small semidetached home at 1126 Chickasaw Drive. It is 1954, and I am seven years old. It is dusk, and the sound of Walter Winchell drips from the blonde wood TV that sits to the right of the chair. I don't understand the words that are on the TV. Something about a guy named McCarthy, and my father is reading the newspaper in the chair, wiping his tortoise shell glasses every now and then to get a clear view of the black and white words he is reading. The pages of the newspaper shuffle as he turns the large sheets from one section to another.

I wish I could change the channel, but my father won't let me. His hands are large, and his fingers are thin, like those of a concert pianist. His brother played for some symphony somewhere in New York, but I don't know where that was, and I have never met his brother. I knew my mother's mother, my grandma, but my father was a mystery. Just like the shadows that crept behind his left ear and covered his right eye. The glasses were thick, and I couldn't see through the lenses to peer into his clear, blue eyes. The eyes that everyone said were just like mine.

His legs rest on the ottoman, and he crosses and uncrosses his feet, which are covered with the brown loafers he always wears. His hair is silver gray and silky. Every few minutes when he turns a page of the paper, his long fingers comb through his silver hair and he brushes the locks from his forehead.

33

That is what I remember. That is all I remember. I don't remember if we took that favorite chair to our new house when we moved. I don't remember talking to my father or saying good-bye to him when he left forever on that fateful Fourth of July weekend six years later. His body was retrieved from the water. That was long after those nights when the TV would spew words I did not understand. I did understand that my father was never coming back and that he had left us. I do remember the lingering shadows on his face and his long fingers turning the pages of the news.

Disappearing Act

*T*he sun is hot. . . very hot. The pavement is soft from the heat. Gravel crunches.

"I'm going to Beverly's house," I announce.

My mother is weeping on the telephone. I see the tears dripping into her enamel coffee cup, the telephone wires wrapped through her fingers and white knuckles.

I leave by the front door, the glare of the noon sun is blinding. I am wearing shorts that ride up my crotch and force me to pull them out of the sticky center. My sneakers catch on the dry grass. My next-door neighbor, Beverly, is waiting in her front porch swing, swaying back and forth. There is shade and ice water. The ice is not yet melted, and there's frost on the milky glass.

"Hi!" Beverly calls. "Dad home yet?"

"Uh-uh," I shake my head. My unwashed curls catch on the sweat of my cheek. Tucking the damp strands behind my ears, I climb and join Beverly on the swing.

Usually we walk on the highway down the hill to the drug store. We sit at the counter and order hot fudge sundaes with whipped cream and a cherry. We wash it all down with Utz potato chips and a cherry coke in a small, five-cent glass.

But today is special. The drug store is closed. It's the Fourth of July, and tonight my Dad will light fireworks bought in Virginia just last week.

My little brother Mike and I have touched the red tissue paper wrapped on cylinders that will explode in the night sky. We stole a forbidden sparkler and lit it after breakfast behind our house.

Mike says to me, "I'll hold the match, and you tip the end of that sparker to the flame until it explodes!"

I do what he says. My heart beats wildly. The sparkler explodes into colored flames. I see that flame twice—once in my hand, and once in the dark pupils under Mike's long lashes. There is fear in my brother's eyes.

Tonight's the night that we'll pull out the cardboard box under the back porch, and my father will say, "You and Mike go stand by the back of the house!"

Mike wants to light the big cones wrapped in tissue with gold stars. I am content to watch. I'm scared of the flames and of the heat. I like to watch the explosions from my safe perch behind the metal fence near the garage door.

Beverly and I swing and sip cold iced water. We watch the sky grow brighter in the July heat.

"Think your Dad is back yet?" Beverly asks. "Probably he's gone to buy more sparklers. We already lit the box in your basement. Hey, wanna see if I have any left?"

"No," I answer. "I'm hungry. Got lunch?"

My father disappeared three days ago. Beverly says he is buying fireworks.

Trixie

When I was thirteen, I lived outside of Washington, D.C. My parents had bought a home on Perth Place instead of the home I wanted them to buy next door to my best friend, Joan. At the last minute, they changed their minds about buying the new house next to Joan. Joan and I had made plans to sleep over each other's houses and to go shopping together at the new Wheaton Plaza, but I never got to live next to Joan.

Instead, we moved to Perth Place. And it was there that, on a fateful Fourth of July, I lost my father to the cold waters of the Potomac River. Late at night his body floated, blue and bloated, along the C&O Canal until it reappeared near Georgetown.

I did not attend the funeral, as my mother didn't think I was old enough. But two days later, my Aunt Janice took my brother and me to buy a dog—a little cocker spaniel with thick paws and red and white spots. She had freckles on her nose, and her name was Trixie. After school (which ended at noon because there were so many of us that the junior high had two sessions) Trixie would run to greet us. We walked to school then. No buses.

The sun would be high in the sky, the maid would have food on the table, and my mother would be "at work." For a year we lived this way, until we didn't. When, at midnight, the song "The Second Time Around" would float into my yellow bedroom through the clouds of darkness, I paid attention.

My mother met a man whom she brought home at night to the

knotty-pine basement with the built-in bar. This is where my father had spent his last sleepless night. My mother was on the sofa with a man I barely knew.

"We are moving," my mother said, just like that. We moved to the home where the man lived with his children. We did bring Trixie. The man and his two kids had a cocker spaniel, too. Her name was Dreamer. The two kids had lost their mother to brain cancer.

The two dogs played in the mud one too many times. We had the dogs until we didn't. Then, they were gone.

"They ran away," my mother told us. She put an ad in the newspaper.

"Lost two small cocker spaniels, If found, call. . . "

One day the phone rang. I answered it. It was cold outside. Snow on the ground. I remember seeing the gray piles of snow lining our driveway out of the window where the telephone sat on the small table.

"BRINNG," the phone said. I picked up the heavy receiver.

"You lost two dogs?" the stranger said.

"Uh-huh," I answered.

"Well," the voice continued, "You ain't gonna find them. Your mother and father let them dogs off on a highway. I saw them open the car door, and I saw them dogs run into the snow, alone. Then, they took off."

Click. The strange voice was gone. I held the cold receiver in my sweating palm.

Loves To Dance

many years later, while I am at work, I receive a call from my husband.

"Come home," he says. "I will drive you to your mother's. I'm so sorry."

I rush for my coat. The rain is heavy on the windshield, and the wipers slosh back and forth to the sound of my pulse.

My mother's apartment is quiet. I immediately spot a sealed envelope left for me on the kitchen counter. Scribbled in large, almost indecipherable print in blue ink is a note—KAREN, spelled out, jumps to my eyes like fireworks, burning and shocking my zombie-like mind.

I grab the letter and rip it open. The glue has dried just hours before.

"Here is a check to pay for the funeral expenses," it reads in the same blue ink. "Pay off my credit cards, also. Here is the key to the safety deposit box at Riggs Bank on 16th Street."

I open the bedroom door. A rancid odor. . . the smell of rotten flesh. . . permeates the gray air.

She is returned to a fetal position, curled tightly on her king-sized bed. The smell of death, the same smell I predicted the night before, drifts to my nostrils.

"She died in her sleep," the police officer explains. It's been about ten hours or so." He tries to explain the putrid air in the darkened room.

We walk to the kitchen, and there the officer takes out his pad. He begins to write in blue ink. I think of my mother's note.

"Heart attack," says the uniformed man, his gold stars twinkling in the morning sunlight. He glances at the still body resting on its side, curled and secure, an older woman dressed in a pink nightgown. He quickly fills out the necessary paperwork, "Date of birth. . . social security number?" he asks me. Soon the heavy front door slams shut. I am alone.

I slip into her rank bedroom and looked around her night table. Sitting like soldiers, lined in rows, eyes at attention were three amber pill bottles, tops off. In the trash nearby were four more bottles, all empty.

She had called my home around eight the night before. We had just finished dinner, and I was tucking my six-year-old into bed. "Here is your brother's phone number in case you need it," she said. I ran to get a pencil and paper and jotted down the seven numbers. I didn't think much about that conversation until just this minute. Now I needed to call my brother right away.

"Mike," I said after my shaky hands dialed his number. "Mom is dead. Come here as soon as you can. This is not a heart attack, trust me." I hung up the receiver attached to its snake-like cord.

I imagine her the night before, taking out a pen and paper from the top drawer of her desk in the office. I imagine her walking into the kitchen and sitting at the round cafe table with two chairs. I see her pondering with her right hand under her chin. "What do I leave to Karen and Mike?" she must have thought. "And what about Gail and Louis?" They were her two stepchildren from this second marriage of twenty-five years.

In the envelope were four checks. Each child received an amount, but not the same amount. She must have given this much thought, as, in a small pile on the table were several checks, torn into small bits. As I rearranged the pieces, I saw that the amounts changed several times before the final product. She left debris to be discarded the next day. A day she would never see. A day she would never realize the consequences of her actions.

My mother could not see herself without a husband.

"You are nothing without a man," she would tell me over and over like a mantra. I was seventeen when she started chanting these words loudly to me.

At sixty-six years of age, there was no light left in her eyes. She was blind to the possibilities that spread before her in the coming months. This moment of death was her future, this time of despair. This time of transition into the loneliness of widowhood was the dead end. My stepfather had died just twelve months before.

As I cleaned her apartment a week later, I found another note. It had been sealed shut with the moisture of her tongue, the taste of her red lips. The note read:

Dear Washington Post Personal Ads:

Woman, 66, widowed, seeks companion of a similar age for travel and laughter. Blonde hair, blue eyes, loves music, loves to dance. . . .

Pennies From Heaven

Soon after my mother died—just a week after, in fact—my son and I were repeating a ritual. Every Friday since Matt could walk, his grandmother took him out for pancakes at Denny's restaurant. Both would look forward to this outing. But, before the pancakes and the maple syrup, my mother would take Matt to the five and dime. There he was able to search the shelves and find just the right toy. He loved this special treat. During the month my mother died, Matt was interested in G. I. Joe dolls. He had garnered quite a collection.

So, on this Friday in November, 1985, I walked into the same five and dime on Flower Avenue with the intent of recreating this experience. I was carrying a green purse that my mother had left behind.

"Matt, let's find a toy for you," I said.

And so he found this G. I. Joe doll dressed in camouflage. It was two dollars and ninety-eight cents.

The reason I remember the price so clearly is that while I was at the checkout counter, Matt's five-year-old palm clutching onto my hand, I tried to pay for the toy.

"You are short two cents," said the young clerk.

"Oh, let me see if I have it."

I searched in the purse, emptied it on the counter. No more change.

"Will you take a credit card?"

"Sorry, we don't take credit for less than five dollars."

"What about a check?"

"Same," she said and yawned.

I looked in my coat pockets. Frantically, we walked out to the car to see if there was a little loose change on the seat or dash. No luck.

I walked back into the store and stood in line again.

"Look," I said, "Can I bring you the two cents in a half an hour?"

"Sorry," she said.

Then I re-examined the purse again. I looked in the bottom again and again. I looked in my wallet and then finally in a pocket of my mother's purse that I had already searched five times. There, tucked in that pocket, was not a nickel or a dime or a quarter. No, there were two pennies!

Now, I often think of this and wonder if they were pennies from heaven. . . or was it that my mother always had to put her two cents in?

art by Jill Pank

IT'S GREAT
BEING A GIRL

Iris

I t's raining, and I am sitting cross-legged on the floor of my cousin Iris's screened in back porch. It smells like mildew because no one ever brings in the green cushions. My favorite comic books, like Little Lucy and Casper and, of course, Archie and Veronica, collect in piles around the porch. I spent many hours alone on the mildewed sofa, reading comics and waiting for my popular, talented cousin Iris to return.

My home is a semidetached townhouse built in the middle fifties. Iris's house is a single-family rambler, also built at the same time, but more expensive. Iris goes to school in a better school district because the dividing line lies somewhere between the blocks that separate our houses. I ride my bike to Iris's home many times, hoping to catch a glimpse of her and her dog Mickey in their front yard.

Iris is a cheerleader and a singer. She once appeared on a TV show, a talent contest. She was wearing her pink poodle skirt and white blouse with the collar turned up. She sang a duet with her best friend. I think she is the most talented, wonderful cousin in the whole world. She sings "How Much Is That Doggie In The Window?" She won third place that day.

Many times when I arrive at her home, the house has a smell of crispy fried bacon. It's noon, and Iris is still in her black and red plaid pajamas. The frying pan sizzles in the small kitchen. Iris carefully drains each slice of bacon on paper and places it on a plate. She moves to her favorite spot on the living room sofa, flips on the TV, and munches her bacon dipped in ketchup. I think that is just too wonderful. Imagine, bacon with ketchup!

I walk to the dining room cabinet and open the hinged doors. There, piled to the sky, are even more mountains of comic books. All of them are there for her to read. So, while Iris dips her bacon in ketchup and tunes into the black and white TV, I stretch out on the living room rug, just loving to be in her house, part of her life.

Iris is eight years older than me. Her phone rings incessantly, ands she has a tight group of best friends and lots of hangers-on who vie for her attention. It's her personality. She's magnetic and funny, and because I am her first cousin and her mother Reva is my aunt, it doesn't matter to her closest friends that I am so young and so chubby. They let me listen to their gossip about Bonnie and her boyfriend Bill.

They go to the movies on Saturday afternoons to see anything with Elvis Presley. Iris loves Elvis, and her entire room is decorated with pictures taken out of magazines like Photoplay and other tabloids. Every single square inch of that room has Elvis's eyes staring out from the wall and the mirrors and even the lampshade.

I don't like Elvis; I like Bullwinkle cartoons and *I Love Lucy*. I don't understand Elvis's appeal. I had a hula-hoop, and once I was in a hula-hoop contest in the parking lot at Lansburg's department store. My hips circled because I wanted to win the contest, not because I wanted to be like Elvis.

Once Iris and I made a record in a little recording booth on the first floor of Lansburg's department store. My voice has no key, but Iris's voice is beautiful. I am thrilled that Iris spends an afternoon with me to make a record, and I can't even sing.

When I tell people who go to Iris's school that I am Iris's cousin, they are impressed. At Christmas Iris gets so many cards that they are strung over her house from one wall to another. Four or five long wires hang in her living room, making the house look like a Chinese Laundry.

I wish I had so many friends.

In high school, Iris plays the lead role in the musical *Oklahoma*. I see the show ten times and learn all the music. As Iris dances on the stage, her voice carries through the auditorium like magic. I love the song "People Will Say We're in Love." I love to sit in the high school gym, night after night, humming along with each scene, enthralled by the costumes, the lights, and the applause. I believe Iris loves me and is proud I am her cousin. This makes me believe, just for a moment, that I am special, too.

Sex And The Schoolgirl

*E*very morning and every afternoon, Debby and I walk the distance to meet our school bus #152. We hold hands, sing and skip to the bus stop. Soon, the familiar yellow and black bus arrives and pumps out its warnings for the other vehicles to wait. We jump on the bus with the other kids who go our elementary school.

The walk home is the best. Chatting and giggling about the day's events, we first stop at my house for an afternoon snack. On this day, I reach under my tee shirt. "I can fill my hand with this mound of boob!" I lift my shirt again to show Debby this miracle. Overnight, my flat chest has sprouted a mountain.

"Look at the nipples," I say. "I think they are redder than they used to be. Darker or something." Next to my pale hand, the nipples flash red and round like the stop sign on the side of the school bus.

"You know what, Debby? Last week when I was in Mrs. Darwin's class. . . . You know Mrs. Darwin? Well, anyway, I was staring at the spelling words on the blackboard when my chair tipped back. The chair touched the desk in this funny kind of way between my legs, and this spot began to tingle."

I remembered that the air in the classroom smelled like dusty chalk and linoleum as I felt the strange but exciting feeling. "It kind of felt like when you ride on a roller coaster, and the hill is a long ride down, and you get this tingling in your tummy that feels real good. You should try it."

We both smile, grab a handful of Oreos and go to the front yard to play our favorite game. . . "A, my name is Alice." We throw the ball against the red bricks in front of my house and the ball bounces on the sidewalk. I am still thinking about my breast and the chilling sensation in Mrs. Darwin's classroom.

"You gonna ask your Mom for a bra?" Deb asks.

"Yes," I answer and toss the ball. "B, my name is Barbara. I live in Boston and I sell BRAS!" I chant.

"Susie has a bra," I tell Debby. Susie lives up the street and is a year older then we are. "She showed me. It was white and stretchy. She said it dug into her shoulders, and it was too small now."

"C, my name is Carol and I sell caramel," Debby chants, tossing the bouncing ball.

"You know what?" I say. "Last week Susie and I touched each other to see if we could get that feeling I told you about. But, you know what? She has straight, black hair down there! Just looking at her hair kind of gave me that feeling again. It felt good. My turn?"

"D, my name is Debby and I live in Denver and I sell dogs," I sing, remembering the sensations that flowed between my legs when I leaned on the desk in Mrs. Darwin's dusty room.

In The Middle

Iris, Lynn and I check into beachfront hotel with no air conditioning. There are fans that blow the leftover sand around the room and feel like grit when we walk on bare feet. Our room is on the third floor, and it is so hot. Sizzling. The air smells of mildew, stale beer, and cigarettes left over, like ghosts that haunt the room from other teenaged parties held over from years of sultry summers.

My cousin Lynn snaps open her round, pink bag and pulls out a powder blue bikini. She has folded it carefully, wrapped it in tissue like a treasure. I watch, trying not to stare, but I am engrossed. Lynn slips the tiny straps over her small, pink breasts, and then the tiny bottom reaches below her waist.

I want to trade my faded red one-piece suit with the stitched skirt for a bikini, one that is trimmed in crisp white lace and will show off the tan that I don't have.

"Lynn, you look beautiful," I whisper worshipfully. Iris is less flashy. But her bright yellow suit highlights her brown skin and glistens against her jet-black hair.

I follow both of them like a trained puppy. They roll their towels, and tuck them under their arms. They carry baby oil mixed with iodine, a transistor radio, and a large blanket. They stumble into the small lobby, hike the splintery boardwalk, and end up on the hot sand.

"Ouch!" I yell.

"Where are your flip-flops?"

"I forgot them."

So we dash over the Sahara-like sand to a cooler spot near the soft surf. We place our blanket with great precision on the sand. Iris is on the left, Lynn is on the right, and I am in the middle. They rub oil on each other's backs. The sun soaks into their skin, and I am pink like a baby armadillo. Lynn and Iris turn golden brown like a baked turkey in a Norman Rockwell painting.

Soon a group of teenaged boys saunters by their blanket. The boys hoot, whistle and wave. They look at each other, smiling with anticipation. The tall one with the sandy hair calls, loudly, so loudly that it echoes in my head over and over. "Hey," he yells, "Who's the fatty in the middle?"

I am in the middle.

When It All Began To Change

For months, my lunch at the Springbrook High School cafeteria is the same. I buy six of the most delicious chocolate chip cookies and two pints of cold milk to wash it down. Sleepy from the bulk that sits in my stomach, I see my afternoon classes drift off in a fog of sugar and lactose. I give up my position on the yearbook, too tired to stay late after the final bell of the day.

I come home to the smell of baked chicken swimming in melted butter. This is our new maid Mary's signature dish. Sometimes crab with cream sauce waits browning in the oven. I grab a spoon from the top drawer, a plate, and eat dinner once at 4:00 PM. Then, when the family eats, I eat again. Dessert is coconut cake with lemon filling, and I eat a hefty slice of that, also.

My mother, now remarried, is the stepmother to Gail, who is my age, and Louis, who is in college but living at home. We have moved into a new home that belonged to the new husband, the house where his ex-wife died of brain cancer just a year earlier.

My new sister Gail is small and athletic. She can enjoy normal portions of food, feel full, and go do her math homework. I hate math. Algebra is an anathema to me. It never makes sense and, besides, it is my last class of the day. My eyes close as soon as I walk into Mr. Porchensky's classroom A113 at the end of the hall. Mr. P. gives me the only "D" on my report card.

This morning I weighed myself for the first time in months. I don't know why it changed, why I wanted to know how much I weighed, why I wanted to stand on that white scale with the little lines that screamed to me. Last time I was on the scale I was 160.

I shower, drop the towel, and gingerly step on the scale... 180. I am in the tenth grade, and have just had my fifteenth birthday. I think of the ice cream and cake, the steak dinner, the twice-baked potatoes, and suddenly, I don't want to be fat anymore. It is a mystery why it all changed.

I slip into my mother bathroom and quietly open her medicine cabinet. She loves pills. All shapes and sizes. Some to sleep, some for pain, and, I think, some for dieting. There are bottles and bottles of pills, and I check each one. There it is: "Tenuate" say the black small letters on the front of the bottle. "Take 1 pill 3x daily for appetite suppressant."

I take off the white plastic top, fill my pocket with a handful of pink, oblong pills, close the bottle, the cabinet door, and slip out of her bedroom. I go to the kitchen sink, and, with one quick gulp of the orange juice waiting for me on the breakfast table, I swallow one of the pills. And wait. Nothing.

The school bus arrives at my front door. Gail and I grab our books and dash to the yellow bus. Still nothing.

I begin to notice that my first period class is different. Mr. Bager is usually so boring, going on and on about geology and the way the rocks shift under the ocean, and who cares anyway. But today, he is fascinating. He shows us a slide show, and my eyes are glued to the screen. My hand scribbles every word he says.

"Wasn't that a great class?" I ask Doreen, my friend who sits next to me in alphabetical order. Her last name begins in "W" also.

"You're kidding, right?" She is bleary-eyed from the long nap she just had. A little bit of drool is falling from the left corner of her mouth and her lipstick is smeared. She represses a yawn, walks beside me to our next class. The morning passes more quickly than usual, and now it is 11:32. The lunch bell rings.

I line up with my other classmates, go to reach for the half dozen cookies, but I am not hungry. I do take one pint of milk and eight saltine crackers. When I go to pay, the lady with the gray hair and the hairnet looks at me with her mouth open.

"This is all you want today?" she asks. "Did ya see the mac and cheese? It's real good today. Crunchy top. The way you like it."

"No thanks," I hear myself answer. I don't know if I can even eat eight saltine crackers. I sit with my usual gaggle of girls."

"Earl Shuster is so cute. I love his white blonde hair," says Sue.

I know who he is, but he never talks to me. He is tall with blue eyes and Aryan splendor. He is on the wresting team, a hero of high school. He is in my algebra class, which is right after lunch. The bell rings, and I am in my seat, alert, book open to page 63. I have just popped the second pill of the day, and my head is spinning. I look at the chalky board. I also sneak a glance at Earl Shuster. He is not looking at me, but he is doing the problems on the blackboard.

"$2x + 6y = 52$ and $19x - 7y = 46$." My eyes are glued to the numbers. They are not Greek today. I understand what Mr. Porchensky is saying for the first time in my class since September. "Wonder why I thought this was so hard," I think as I close the dusty book, tuck away my sharpened pencil in its little plastic bag. Again the bell rings. Two hours later, the school day is over. For once, I am not tired.

By the time I reach home, my heart is racing like a strong summer wind. I think maybe Mary can hear the sound, but she acts the same as always.

"Hi!" I call out to her.

"You sure are happy today," she calls up from the basement, where the smells of pressed cotton drift like tide on soft sand. I turn on the TV and dance with American Bandstand.

Gail and I do the pony. "You're getting better at this," smiles Gail, and we then do the twist to the music blaring from the TV.

I pass the kitchen with the chocolate cake and the smell of melted butter and head to my desk to do my math homework. Gail peeks in my room.

"You're doing MATH?" She squeals. "I can't believe it. Do you want help?"

"No, I can do it myself tonight," and I finish the twenty problems before dinner. I'm having fun when I pop the third pill before dinner,

"What's wrong?" asks my brother Mike. "You sick or something?" My plate has a teaspoon of salad, a drop of peas, and a tiny bit of chicken. I can barely finish.

"No, I'm fine," I answer, but I notice my hand is shaking a bit. The peas fall off of the fork and drop to the kitchen floor. Our dog, Trixie sniffs the peas, rejects them, and I bend down to pick them up.

"Well, how come you're not grabbing for food?" asks my brother as he swallows a huge bite of mashed potatoes smothered in the melted butter.

"Dunno," I answer. I patiently wait until dinner is over. I don't want to draw attention to myself. "I'm going back to finish my homework," I say, and I work until Ben Casey, MD comes on. Gail and I think he is so handsome.

"Look at that chest," she sighs. I look at his hairy chest, his brown eyes, his stethoscope, and for the first time I notice he has a dimple in his chin. "Funny, I never saw that before," I think as we turn off the TV and get ready for bed.

Usually, as soon as I hit the pillow, I am gone. But, tonight, I can't sleep. The minutes pass, and when I look at the alarm clock shining brightly in the dark room, it is 2:00 AM.

"I'll be so tired tomorrow," I think. But the next morning, after I swallow another of those pink pills with water, not juice, I am ready for geology again. Doreen already has her head on her desk, anticipating her morning nap. I can't wait for Mr. Bager's lesson to begin.

Nose Job

"Daddy, Daddy!" A voice calls from underwater. It sounds familiar, and I have heard the voice before.

Wait. . . the voice is mine. I am pushed on a gurney to an operating room, a blue nurse, efficient and cold, pushing and pushing. I can't stop the damn thing.

'No! NO! Stop!" I plead. Then. . . Nothing. I wake in the operating room, eyes bleary and mind unfocused. The scrunch and crack of a broken bone, the whirrs of a drill, and a hammering, bang! Bang! Banging on my nose. I am fifteen and scared, terrified, in fact. I am in the Twilight Zone and the pig-faced people are staring at me. Just like the Rod Serling episodes.

"Ohhh," I moan. The medical team, shower caps on their heads, gowns wrapped around their bodies like death shrouds, glare at me. The silver, shiny instruments gleam wickedly under the fluorescent lights, which blind me.

"You OK in there?" asks one of the ghosts.

"NO!" I moan. "Take me home! Daddy! Daddy!"

Then, nothing.

When I awaken, it is dark and I am in a hospital room. I have to pee. I lift my head, now a ton of concrete on my shoulders. I drag my heavy body off of the hospital sheets, traipse on the cold tiled floor to the bathroom, which I find like a bomb dog, following the perfumed scent of rubbing alcohol and ether.

Sitting on the cold toilet, I stare at the door in front of me.

Then. . . nothing. I am flat on the floor, my face on the frozen tiles. The nurse hears the bang and runs into the bathroom.

"What happened?" she asks.

The night nurse is warm. "Here honey, let me help you," she says as she cajoles me onto my feet and assists me to my bed.

"Here," she says, placing a buzzer into my teenaged palm. "If you need anything, a drink, maybe, just ring for me. I'll be right here."

My mother arrives the next morning, her nose is perfect, and her hair is shellacked and sprayed by Jimmy, her favorite hairdresser.

"Hi, Sweetie. . . here is an ice cream for you."

I take the cold treat and place it between my parched lips. I can't swallow.

"You're gonna look great," she says brightly. "Dr. Juneau says the stitches will come out in a week. You can come home tomorrow. I can only stay an hour, and then I have my mahjongg game. It's Tuesday, remember?"

My old nose is gone, gone, gone. My mother insisted on the bump leaving my face. No sign of Semitism, and perfect symmetry.

"You have such lovely blue eyes," she says. "Your nose was ruining your beauty."

She found the plastic surgeon in the yellow pages and drove me to the hospital in her mauve Bonneville.

"Daddy!" I had called as they whirled me into surgery. But, of course he could not hear me or save me. He had been dead for two years.

Boundaries

I started seeing Dr. Jewell when I was twenty-two. All boundaries were crossed. I had no idea of boundaries, correct or incorrect. That was the biggest lesson I had to learn. How do I set boundaries for myself and others?

I found Dr. Jewell through my friend Betty. His office was on Connecticut Avenue in D.C., and I lived in Georgetown with my cousin Iris. I went to see him every week. I took a teaching job so I could have insurance to pay for my sessions. I joined a therapy group in Annapolis. When I was interviewing for my job, I told my principal that I would have to have a sub every Thursday morning so I could drive to Annapolis and be in a group from 9:00 AM to noon. The drive to Annapolis was over an hour and then I would drive back to work, another one and a half hours.

I was totally addicted to this process. My cousin Susan began seeing Dr. Jewell. Soon she began dating him. He brought her to his home in Annapolis and slept with her. He invited Susan and me to join him to see his son perform in a play in Virginia. I went with him and Susan. His wife was taking the tickets. We walked right past her.

After I was married, I began to see Dr. Jewell again. I joined a therapy group that met in his yard by the river in Virginia. On dark, smoky nights we sat by a fire, all ten of us. The campfire sparked while the toasted marshmallows caramelized. It was August, and the lingering buzz of cicadas drowned out the chatter. Dr. Jewell was presiding over the group, nodding his white goateed chin this way or that to indicate attention and approval.

I admired Dr. Jewell. His blue eyes sparkled, and laughter filled the circle that separated him from me. His trailer was on the side, and while others slipped to their Spartan tents, he nodded to me. I knew I would follow him into the cushy space. When I entered, there was vodka in shots already lined on the counter. The music played softly from the 8-track recorder. Already playing, but it seemed so wonderful to me. I loved Dr. Jewell's insights, the joint that had been passed around the circle after the baked beans but before the coleslaw. I was intoxicated by his power.

He tipped his chin towards the bed that was covered in a soft lambskin. It looked inviting, and I wanted to go there with him. I wanted to find myself completely naked and vulnerable, enjoying more intimacy than any of the other members of the group enjoyed. I was special, and I slipped out of my shorts and removed the tee that clung to me just so. I felt blessed. The stars were winking at me. I winked back.

Faceman

Dr. Money is the "faceman" in Sarasota, Florida. He used to do breasts, and still does if you happen to have a relationship with him. But, for his new patients, he is only a "faceman." He works wonders for the matrons of Sarasota. He is an expert in Botox, collagen, lips, eyes, necks, and whatever.

He wanted to be an artist, but his parents explained that that was a "back-up" job. He combined his interest in art with his interest in money and medicine and became a plastic surgeon.

Most women in Sarasota who frequent the office of Dr. Money are wealthy or married to wealthy men. I learned this information from Susie, his receptionist. Susie lives close to my home and regales me with tales of Dr. Money.

Susie has been his patient for the ten years she has worked for him. Dr. Money has a "self-improvement" day for his office help. The three women who work with Susie get to have a wish list. And, once a month each gets their wish fulfilled for free.

Susie explains, "Last month I wanted new breasts and a tummy tuck. So, Jake (Dr. Money) gave me my dream. See, my new breasts?"

She unbuttons her shirt and shows me her new breasts. They are perky and large.

"My stomach was done, also." Susie explains. She shows me her navel.

"Look at this," she says as she points to her abdomen. "See this bellybutton? Dr. Money replaced my navel. This is the new one. I had it pierced." I wonder what happened to the old one, but I don't ask.

With that, Susie displays her beautiful diamond stud she had pierced into her new navel. Then, she shows me her breast again. "See," she points out, "The breasts are tan. I had my entire body painted tan with this new brush technique. You stand in a room, and the tanning solution is sprayed on. No tanning bed. Perfectly safe. Don't I look great?"

"Wow," I answer. "Yes, you do."

Her body looks perfect. Just like a super model. Her stomach is flat. Her navel is decorated. Her waist is tiny. Susie's face is perfect, also. She is forty-five but looks thirty. Not a wrinkle. Her lips are full. Her nose is aquiline. Her eyes are bright. She had her lips tattooed with pink and her eyes permanently lined with black. She is a work of art.

If you ever come face-to-face with Susie, you would never know that her perfect features and her perfect body are not natural.

"Yes," she emphatically states, "Dr. Money is a genius. Women from all over the world come to Sarasota to be his patients. Some of the women are very famous, but I can't reveal their names. Confidentiality, you know. Do you want the number of his office? I could fit you in next week?"

I look in the mirror on a daily basis and come face-to-face with my age. My wrinkles, my abdomen, my thighs. . . maybe I should get Dr. Money's phone number! Only Susie and Dr. Money would know.

Nancy Reagan Arms

"Give thanks for something greater than yourself," says Jaye, the yoga teacher. His hands are in the prayer mudra. His head is bent in soulful fashion. Jaye stretches, bends, and coils his body like a telephone cord. Our class stares in awe at his gyrations.

"There is no prize for touching your toes. No cookie on the floor." Jaye repeats time and time again.

I can't help myself. I peek at the person to the left and the right. If there were a cookie, it would be in their mouths, chewed and swallowed before my fingers could reach the wooden floor."

"Nowhere to go, no hurry," repeats Jaye

Vicky, in front of me on a purple mat, can fold like cookie dough, roll her spine and swing her lithesome arms to the floor. She is grace.

I am stiff. My tendons have forgotten the joy of youth. and my legs are buried in cement.

"My hamstrings are so tight," I think, as I watch my classmates sway like wild branches. I see myself as the brittle, black tree in November, bare branches snapping in raw winter wind.

Now Jaye explains, "There is no getting 'there.' Only the Here and Now...." He smiles his Mona Lisa smile, the one that is indecipherable.

Hey... wait... what is he saying now? I must be mistaken. "Stretch your triceps," he says. "You don't want Nancy Reagan arms, do you?"

I stop mid-air. I think. Nancy Reagan? I try to remember her arms in her red gowns, standing next to Ronnie at the White House balls.

Yes, now I recall. I can see her off-the-shoulder number, her skin drooping off the bone underneath her slender limbs. Her triceps are not toned!

"Oh, NO!" I think. "I don't want Nancy Reagan arms."

And, now the class is swaying this way and that way, and I am still at the White House with Nancy and Ron and the Ambassador from India. His wife is wearing a sparkling green sari and there she is… Nancy, in red, her arms swaying in the breeze like the flaps on a leather saddle.

Yep, Nancy Reagan has "Nancy Reagan arms."

The class is over. "Bow to your teachers, bow to your heart, bow to a power greater than yourself," Jays instructs.

I bow. I think of Nancy. I have been stopped dead in my tracks. Is there a power greater than myself who can help me escape the "Nancy Reagan arms" fate?

I hope so. I joined the YMCA.

Abundance Scam

*E*llen has written and published her own book, Starlight. I bought it from her, as she carries copies with her all the time. She signed the book for me.

I also bought her dinner at the Main Street Bistro, as she is short on money. She constantly complains about how poor she is. At the time of the dinner on Main Street, she had a job at the BPA, a very exclusive private school here in Sarasota that pays little. I felt sorry for her and for her financial situation.

A year has passed since the Main Street dinner, and today I am sitting in front of her little temple she has installed in her spare bedroom. We are chanting, and she is explaining her newfound religion.

"I am a Jew-Boo," she says. "That is a Jew who has turned Buddhist."

Pointing to the spot where the lotus lies on the scroll within the small cabinet, she explains, "Look at this spot and envision what you want."

I chant. I stare. I envision. I see myself twenty pounds thinner and toned. I am attending Weight Watchers, and I am struggling with a difficult yoga class. I go to the gym twice a week and work with free weights. I am acting as well as visualizing.

Ellen shows me the list of intentions she has placed on her altar.

"I want a new body."

"I want an abundance of money."

"I want to sell many copies of my book."

And so on.

Ellen starts to cry. She is leaving town to babysit for a relative who has a dog and a cat. They will pay her $200. This is for a month.

Ellen has her name on all of the substitute teaching lists in town.

Last week, she was offered a long-term sub job at a minority high school. The class was tough.

"I hate those kids," she complains. "I won't teach those idiots. I won't waste my time. It makes me miserable."

Now, long-term sub jobs pay more than the one-day jobs. I remember the last five years of teaching at a difficult high school. So much of the job was policing.

"I hated my job, also," I tell her. "But I stuck it out for the last five years. I wanted that pension."

I say to Ellen, "Hey, sometimes you got to do what you got to do."

"DON'T SAY THAT!" she explodes.

She quit the long-term job and waited for the exclusive private school to call. That school pays half the money the public school pays. The kids are clean and wealthy.

Ellen chants three nights a week and hangs out at Starbucks most of the days of the week. She complains about money.

She tells me as we have finished chanting, "Tommy offered money. I told him to wait until the summer when I am really desperate."

She begins to sob, her tears spilling from her eyes. "I don't take loans. I can't pay them back. My friends and relatives write checks and drop them in my purse." She begins to sob more. "I hate that. It makes me feel like shit."

"Am I supposed to look for her purse?" I think as I watch her cry.

We return to her living room. She is arranging all of the jewelry she bought last year on the QVC shopping channel. There must be hundreds of bracelets, rings, and earrings. Three jewelry boxes full of "bling-bling."

"Did you buy all of this?" I ask, thinking perhaps it was inherited from her mother or something like that.

"Yeah," she answers. "Last year when I had that job, I went a little crazy."

Last year I was treating her to lunches, dinners and movies. Offering her free tickets to shows. I wanted to help her.

Today, I feel like a sucker. Ellen is as talented as a modern day beggar as she is as a writer. I guess I am seeing through her scam. Too bad she can't see through her dilemma.

Shiva

In the Jewish faith, it is called a "Shiva," and that is what Bobbie didn't want when her husband Fred died. Nothing. "I hated him," she said. "Why would I want to honor him?" Friends called and called until finally Bobbie decided to do something. "Come next Wednesday night," she said. "Bring something to eat."

Some of us brought cheese, and others brought crackers. Some of us brought fruit, and others brought cake. We all wanted something for closure so we could rest at night and not feel that Fred had drifted into infinity with nothing to mark his birth or his death. Some of us sent cards, and some of us gave donations to local organizations. We all looked forward to the Shiva being held at Bobbie's home in Pinecrest Village. We all dressed in fine clothes, and we all powdered our noses. Some of the men wore collared shirts and switched out their shorts for long khakis. Some even wore closed toe shoes instead of flip-flops to mark the occasion.

We all pulled into the driveway, some in our convertibles and some in our SUVS. We switched off the engines and filed into Bobbie's somber home. All the chairs were set in a circle, and we placed our offerings on the dining table. Some of us saved seats for our spouses, and some of us didn't. Some of us put a sweater around our shoulders, and others took our jackets off. We perused the photos Bobbie had on display. The pictures showed Fred at thirty years, or forty or even seventy. No photos showed him within the last five years. We waited for Bobbie to speak. We waited for her to tell us something beautiful about Fred, whom some of us had not seen in years. He had taken to his bed and barely moved for a long time.

Bobbie began to speak. We expected sorrow, and we expected tears. But this is what we got. "I never liked him," she said. "I only stayed for the money, and even that wasn't worth it. I never had fun with him, and I never wanted to be with him, except for the sex, which was OK, some of the time. Now I am worried about my financial future, but I certainly won't miss him. Not for a second."

Then she sat still. We were stunned and dismayed. We all were silent. We looked at one another, and then each of us stood and began to walk out the door. Even the food was left untouched. No one said "goodbye." Only the sound of car doors slamming. On the branches, the birds continued their evening songs, and the squirrels scampered up and down the thick trunks of trees on the lawn. The engines started, and each of us waited our turn to leave.

Riding Shotgun

$\mathcal{J}$asmine Wentworth was born with a silver spoon in her mouth. Everything she ever wanted could be paid for with her mother's credit card. She wore glass slippers on her size nine feet that fit her just fine until she ran into a cement wall. That's when her slippers splintered into shards, and that damn silver spoon was shoved down her throat until she could no longer breathe.

Yep, those glass slippers fooled the world, but the facts were different. The rehab was a glamorous glitzy place, a quick right turn off of Route 101. In fact, her bedroom was in Kelsey Grammar's old house, the one he owned before he married Beverly Hills housewife, Camille. There was an infinity pool, and the sunrise broke over the never-ending rippling water.

Everyone she saw was stunning. Blonde and tall, willowy and healthy, young and happy. That was the thing, everyone was happy. The patients were grateful to be there, but struggling with their addictions to alcohol, sex, and drugs, to money and to excess, addicted to false realities that had hung on each of them like barnacles on a loggerhead turtle.

One man owned a tremendous amount of real estate and flew in to California as the pilot of his own plane.

"Yeah," he told her, "I love to fly high. I love to chew fentanyl patches and soar into the clouds." His limo rested outside the marble entrance day and night, waiting to see what he wanted to do on any given moment of the thirty-day period he had signed up for. The cost was seventy thou a month, but his assistant was already filing paperwork for reimbursement from Blue Cross/Blue Shield. He was sure that she would figure it out. He didn't expect to be out-of-pocket for any of the expense.

Jasmine visited the koi fish swimming in the pond at the front entrance. She got to know them and named each after her favorite celebs. One was Cameron and another, Charlie. The friendly swimming couple were Brad and Angie, and their baby was Maddox. He looked slightly Asian.

There was a masseuse and an acupuncturist and hypnotist and a personal trainer. There were yellow plastic bracelets in an antique Ming china bowl in the cavernous lobby. Each bracelet had the word "PERFECT" imprinted. Life was perfect, and everythig happened for a reason. The owner, Charles, had written his Buddhist philosophy in the books sold at the front desk for twenty dollars each. Yes, the world was perfect. This world.

Alone in her room, away from the glittering perfect exterior, Jasmine tried to stop the sun from rising. This was a great lesson. She couldn't stop the rising dawn from breaking through the dark. She didn't want the sun to rise. She didn't want the gardeners to start their blowers, and she didn't want the uniformed maids to vacuum her room or rouse her out of the down comforters.

And, in the midst of all this glamour, there in high def, was Khloe Kardashian. Jasmine was living in Kardashian country right on the mountains of Malibu, in the midst of the world's most prime real estate. Every night, alone with her 60-inch TV and her remote control, she tuned into "E" channel, displayed on the menu that magically appeared on the screen before her.

Khloe Kardasian, a member of the celeb-driven reality sister team of Kim and Kourtney, was dressed in a lovely gown. Her wedding rolled every night, every single night, for the four weeks that Jasmine lived in her room that overlooked the wealthy shores of Malibu. Every night, every single night, Jasmine watched as Khloe picked out her gown at Vera Wang. She watched Khloe have the same argument with Bruce Jenner, her stepfather. She watched Khloe curl her subtle body around the black muscles of basketball star fiancé, Lamar Odom.

Jasmine wasn't happy at all, but Khloe and Lamar were so happy. Their world was one of endless possibilities. Maybe that's why she couldn't stop watching the TV. She watched the same show, over and over, time and time again, hypnotized for two hours from eight to ten every night—every single night, for thirty days. There, before her searching eyes, was her secret fantasy, two beautiful people, two paper doll figures, winding their lives together to form the perfect union. Never would they be alone. Never would they suffer. They were on the road to happy-ever-aftering, and Jasmine was riding shotgun with them.

art by Jill Pankey

YOU'RE NOTHING WITHOUT A MAN

Follow The Man

On Wednesday nights every week, my mother and father would disappear after dinner. Collar turned up with a wide belt taut, my mother's shirtwaist dress was ironed just so. She would give instructions to Wilma and leave while I watched Lucy bicker with Desi on the *I Love Lucy* show. My brother and I would stretch out on the sofa until our toes touched and fight with our feet as the TV blared over our screams.

The next night, after dinner and after the evening news, my father would teach me to do the Mambo. I would run to the knotty pine rec room with the built-in bar and the mirrored wall. Behind that bar was storage for piles of my broken toys, marking the transition from Tiny Tears to Barbie Dolls.

Placing the vinyl recording on the turntable, my dad would beckon me to join him in dance. Soon the sound of Latin nights would bounce off the cavernous walls, reach from right to left, under and over, and spill like rum and coke on the spotted linoleum floors.

My father's shoes would glide, black and shiny, as if we were skating on ice.

"Follow me," he would direct, placing his arm around my chubby waist and executing the "one-two, one-two-three" dance steps he had learned the night before. "Always follow the man," he would instruct, and I would struggle to get the steps right, turning when he gave me the signal to move my feet with the rhythm of the slippery music.

"That's good," he would comment, his black-framed glasses masking his eyes while the fluorescent light from the ceiling sparkled in his silver hair. The music would play, and I would glide to the touch of my father's hand as I learned to follow the man.

Dress Rehersal

I am standing with my back to the Atlantic Ocean, my hand in my father's, my brother and mother forming bookends around our cocoon. I'm wearing a "party dress." It's turquoise with a white ruffled collar, and a black velvet ribbon for a waistband.

This is my favorite dress. I wore it when I "married" Larry, the cute boy across the street from our home. I was six and he was seven, and we planned the whole ceremony. I was the "daughter-in-training." This was my dress rehearsal for my future as a wife. This was one of the few times I can remember my mother showing interest in any of my projects. Mostly my mother was on the phone chatting to her best friend, Janice, playing mahjongg, or having her hair done once a week at the beauty shop. Sometimes my mother would work with my father in his business or go shopping with her friends. Catching my mom's attention was exciting. I was a bride.

There would be flowers from our garden, linen tablecloths from the front closet, and ten of my best friends. Debby, Doreen, and Larry's little sister, Barb, would sit at the "head" table. They would eat hot dogs and hamburgers cooked by Wilma in the backyard. There would be a red Jello mold shaped like a heart as a centerpiece. Canned fruit would float inside of the cherry confection like fish in a still ocean, topped with waves of whipped cream. My favorite.

Wilma would bake the cake." What color do you want the icing?"

I checked with Larry.

"White with pink roses."

Wilma asks, "How about the cake? Chocolate or vanilla?"

I check with Larry again, always the acquiescent young "bride-in-training."

"Vanilla," I tell Wilma.

Then my mother and I go shopping for the "Dress." I hold my mother's attention for days. We search through the local department stores—Jelleff's, Hecht's and Woody's. We go to the children's boutiques in Silver Spring Shopping Center and find other stores in Langley Park. I try on dress after dress until finally a turquoise transparent fabric peeks through the racks.

"Oh," I say to my mother, "I like that one."

My mom inspects the delicate fabric, the white collar, and the price.

"This is pretty," she says. "Here, try it on."

We go to the tiny dressing room and the salesgirl helps me slip it on. I feel the slippery fabric slide over my smooth skin. It molds to my body and hugs my thick waist.

As I step out to the carpeted area in front of the store, several customers turn around, smiling and nodding their well-coiffed heads. I turn, taffeta crinoline swishing back and forth in front of the tall, three-sided mirror.

"Do you like it?" I ask.

My proud "mother-of-the-bride" beams. "It's perfect. We'll take it." The dress is wrapped in pink tissue paper, tied inside with a satin ribbon. The box is pink with a turquoise bow.

We carry the package home and place it on the dining table.

"Now, don't show Larry your dress," my mother instructs. "The groom never sees the dress before the wedding." And so, for a week, I stare at the unopened box, waiting, endlessly waiting for the big day when I can wear my special dress and eat Wilma's vanilla cake.

Nothing Without a Man

*W*hen my mother told me, "You're nothing without a man," I believed her.

"Marry him," my mother said. "Marry Jay. He has a great business. What do you mean you want to go away to college? The University of Maryland is good enough for you. You don't need Antioch or Berkeley. I'll buy you a silver fastback Mustang with wire wheels. Go to Maryland and join a sorority. Maybe you will meet a man. . . a nice Jewish man. Be a teacher so that you can have the same hours as your kids."

My mother told me, "Marry Jay! Why look any further? I know you are only eighteen, but he can take care of you. Don't break up with him. Please, go out with him one more time. You want the blue Villager outfit? Fine. You can have the green one, too, with the knee socks and the matching round collared blouse. Just go out with Jay. He is fine marriage material."

I don't marry Jay, but I do go to the University of Maryland instead of Antioch or Berkeley. I drive the silver Mustang with the wire wheels and the hatchback. I pledge a sorority and look for a husband. I'm not interested in my work. I feel small and lonely. I don't have a boyfriend.

I live on the eighth floor of Denton Hall. My roommate is Anne. One night Anne and I hear Lois calling from her room. Lois is sprawled bare-chested across her bed. "I can make my nipples hard just thinking about it."

We all stare at Lois's erect nipples and watch them grow even larger with each passing moment. I wonder what is going on in her head. What is she thinking about?

Lois continues, "I can have an orgasm too. I just have to think about it long enough!

I think of Lois's nipples and I remember my mother's voice. The power of the mind is amazing. My mother's message echoes deep in my brain. Over and over my mother's voice repeats, "You're nothing without a man."

What More Is There?

I am twenty-six years old and in love. Josh is the man who will make my life complete. I just know it.

On a bright Sunday morning, we visit his sister Sally in her perfect home. It's a brunch, and her two kids are running around the house; the neighbors are dropping in for "hellos," and I am part of this suburban domestic scene. Joints, dreadlocks and Birkenstocks are far behind me now, left somewhere in Georgetown with the drugs, the Eagles, and my grandmother's old sofa.

Sally's home has distressed barnwood on one wall that envelops the fireplace. The furniture is draped in bright chintz. Fresh flowers are delivered daily to her house for baskets of color around the home. Over the kitchen counter is a little sign made for her by her husband—"Sam loves Sally." We eat smoked salmon and bagels, hot scrambled eggs on good china. The coffee is steaming, and the cream is cold and thick. Martha Stewart is not yet known, but if Sally didn't have those two kids, she would be a candidate for the job.

"Sam is head of oncology at Beth Shalom Hospital," Josh tells me. "He is difficult and overpowering, so Sally works hard to please him."

"I think he's adorable," I say, as Josh has been holding my hand and rubbing my back while we watch the Sunday football game. All the men in the family are huge sports fans. The wives chat and cook. The men cheer for the Redskins. This is a typical Sunday, and I want to be part of this life.

I don't want to cry on the sofa of my living room, pining away for Eddie and his stupid gold earrings. The joints and the bong can stay in Georgetown. I am ready for a change.

Josh and I climb into his car and head back to his apartment. He is silent.

"What are you thinking?" I say.

"I love you."

"But we just met last week. . . I love you too."

"Will you marry me?"

"When?"

"In June." It's now the end of January. I haven't met his parents. He doesn't know my family. Eddie thinks I am still dating him.

"Well," I say, "I have to break up with Eddie. Then, yes, I will marry you."

The next day, we are in Georgetown, and I'm on the phone with Eddie.

"So listen," I am saying. "I met someone over the weekend, and I am going to get married. Do you want those earrings back?"

"Married?" he says.

"Yep!"

"That was quick," he comments sarcastically. "Keep the earrings. Bye."

Now I am free. Free to marry Josh and meet more of his family. His mother who decorates; his father, with whom he shares a business; and his brother, Jerry, his twin. This family unit sounds perfect. Just what I have dreamed about.

I will have a beautiful home like Sally, children who run around the kitchen table. Soon, I will be Mrs. Karen Kerry. Cute name. Just perfect. Sounds like a cheerleader.

How 'bout Them Skins?

"Do you have any quarters?" asks my fiancé, Josh. It's 1973, and a beautiful warm glow fills the apartment we share as lovers on a sunny winter afternoon.

"I think so," I answer, reaching for my wallet and handing him eight shiny quarters. "How many do you need?"

"Only two," he murmurs. "I'm going to do just a quick load of whites." I hand Josh the change, and he carries the laundry out of the third-floor apartment to the laundry room at the end of the hall.

I think of our wedding in June, about how comfortable it is to share my life with this man. I am starry-eyed at twenty-six years and have spent many nights dreaming of this person who has magically come into my life.

Meanwhile, the Redskins are close to winning the Superbowl this year. We have the den ready for the big Sunday game. The popcorn is popped and warm, butter melting in a small pot on a slow heat. The beer is chilling, and the cheese is just about room temperature. We are minutes away from kickoff. I don't like football, but I do love Josh, and I love the family feeling of this enchanted Sunday afternoon.

"Hurry up!" I call to him as he tugs at the door to open it with one hand, lugging the bag of laundry in the other.

"Do you want some help?" I ask.

"No, no, I'm fine. See you in a sec," and he slams the door behind him.

Two hours later, I am frantic. Every five minutes I walk to the door and peek out. No, Josh. I go to the laundry room and find that an impatient tenant has removed his wet laundry and placed it on the top of the dryer. The whirring sound of the washing machine in the rinse cycle is bouncing off the walls, reminding me that Josh has been gone for hours.

I have eaten the Boursin cheese, walked again to the laundry room, crunched most of the Ritz crackers. I walk to the laundry room again. Now the dryer is banging with another's laundry, and Josh's wet, white clothing is still on the top.

I put the beer back in the fridge after drinking three Coronas. I sit by the phone and wait for a ring. Nothing. Silence. I watch the clock on the oven move slightly. Now it's half-time, and the Redskinettes are bouncing while the white stripes on the field are glaring through the darkening room.

I walk to the grocery store on the ground level and march up and down the aisles.

"Hey, Joe," I ask, trying to be nonchalant, but shivering inside. "Have you seen Josh? Did he stop by to buy some chips or something?"

"Nope," says Joe. "But it's a hell of a game, isn't it? How 'bout them Skins?"

Back into the elevator, up to the third floor, check the laundry room, which is now silent, with wet clothing sitting in a heap like soggy ghosts.

Finally, I check the parking lot. I search for his car, thinking maybe he left. But no, his car is still in its assigned space, innocently resting for the Monday morning run to work.

Only hours ago Josh said to me, "I love you." He says this over and over, hugging me and kissing my neck as I scramble the eggs and fry the bacon. The comforting smell of smoky bacon is still in the air as the door opens. The game is in the fourth quarter.

"I just put the wet laundry in the dryer," he tells me, as if nothing has happened. As if I had not spent the last hours with my stomach aching, my heart pounding loud enough to be heard through the solid apartment walls.

"Where were you?" I scream.

"Calm down," he answers as if this were the most normal behavior in the world. "I ran into Steve and Barb, and they invited me over to see their new furniture and have a drink. Was I gone that long? I must have lost track of the time."

I am so relieved to see him, so stunned by his disappearance, I am silent. I don't want to see a crack in my perfect dream. My wedding is in two months. The dress, the invitations, the presents all await. The future is mine. It isn't until years later that I learn where he was that day when the Redskins won the playoffs and made it to the Superbowl.

First Home

It was 1976, and I had been married two years. I wanted a family, a dog, and a baby. Josh had two children from his previous seven-year marriage. One boy was four years old, and the other was six. Josh was not ready for another family yet, but he would agree to the dog and the house.

On a bright spring day, I found a real estate agent, and I called her. This was my first foray into the world of residential real estate. I was a young bride in my twenties.

"Do you have anything in the $60,000 range?" I asked.

"This means Silver Spring," the agent said, as if it were Outer Mongolia. I grew up in Silver Spring. At that time, it was the Jewish enclave. Temple Israel was just two blocks away. That was where I would go for the High Holy Days in my warm clothes and heels on hot September days.

"What about Takoma Park?" I asked. This area was gentrified. It was the bastion of intellectual artist-types, consignment stores, and yoga studios, Birkenstock shoes and peace protests. It was the Park Slope of D.C. suburbia.

The real estate agent answered, "I know just the place. Flower Avenue. It begins in Silver Spring and is only a mile away from Takoma Park. The neighborhood is filled with young families, dogs, and playgrounds."

I pictured myself strolling hand-in-hand with my handsome new husband. He would be holding the leash of our golden retriever, and I would be pushing the stroller to the nearby park on weekend mornings or summer evenings.

There were sidewalks where we could safely ride our bikes and mature trees that cast cozy shadows on the grassy lawns and clapboard shutters.

"Here, hop in," said the agent.

Going to see the house, we drove miles on Route 495, the beltway that surrounded Washington, D.C. Here was the YMCA that used to be Indian Spring Country Club. Our family, along with every other middle-class Jewish family, belonged to this country club in the fifties. When the club was in its heyday, there were swimming lessons and tennis courts; there were golf courses and lunch in a fly-filled screened-in porch. I could see the old club as we drove past. Now the golf course was gone, new homes built on all eighteen holes.

We turned onto Flower Avenue, and the agent took me into this small red brick colonial home built in 1937. The home had a cozy living room and dining room and a small kitchen on the first floor. Upstairs were three bedrooms and one bath. The basement was paneled, and there, next to the laundry room, was another bath.

The house felt like chocolate-chip cookies and apple pie. I imagined that under the powder blue carpet were wooden floors. Someday the kitchen would be expanded, and the garage would become a child's playroom and a family den.

"I'll take it," I said. "But, I need to have my husband Josh drive over."

The agent called Josh at the office and gave him directions, and he was at the house in a half an hour. I watched him walk up the three front steps that led to the red wooden door with the brass knocker. I was excited. I hoped this would be the first of many homecomings.

Josh said, "You won't believe this. . . See that white house across the street?"

I walked to the window and looked at another house very much like the one we were visiting. This house had white painted brick and black shutters. "Our" house was red brick with green striped awnings and a small side screened-in porch. "Our" house had purple and pink hydrangeas and forty-year-old azaleas. In the backyard was a huge oak tree that must have been sixty years old. The roots were like the tangles of an octopus, springing up from the earth with hosta planted in the shade under the huge limbs.

"Yes," I said, "I see that house. Why? Do you like it better than this one?" I was disappointed and holding my breath.

"No," he answered. "That is the house where I was born and where our family lived until I was twelve. I loved growing up here. It's a great neighborhood. It feels just like home."

We bought the house. Our son, Matt, was born there. Our golden retriever's name was Lindsey. We took long walks in the park on Sunday afternoons after the lawn was mowed and the weeds were pulled. Maybe a turkey or a meatloaf with baked potatoes would be cooking in the oven. Red juicy tomatoes waited on the counter to be sliced.

We lived in that house for twelve years. I loved that house. It made me feel like I was on the Ozzie and Harriet show.

The Bowles Thing

ost Americans don't give a rat's ass about the Royal Family, but I do. As an avid reader of every gossip tabloid since I was ten, I watched Lady Diana fall in love with Charles. I saw them at the river in Sandringham, both in tweed, when the interviewer asked Charles if he was in love. His answer, a meek, "Well, whatever that is, yes, I suppose," or something moldy like that. It was shocking. Milquetoast.

When I saw the sun between her beautiful gauzy legs, when the photo was backlit through thin cotton, I thought she was beautiful. And beautiful when she wore that black strapless number to the opera and her breasts fell out of it because she was so round and full and lovely at the time. She, of course, fell asleep at the opera. As we all knew, she wasn't particularly intellectual.

I watched her wedding, the pomp and circumstance, the horses and the feathers, the gilded lilies and all. I saw her thin neck reach like a swan to kiss the mouth of Charles who held his distance just a bit too far and made her stretch to kiss his Royal lips, sword at his side, kilt swinging in the breeze.

I watched her get thinner and thinner, glossier and glossier. I saw her through both of her pregnancies, browsed through tons of photo books, the coffee table types in Barnes & Noble, admiring her taste in clothes and sheer beauty. Her hair was a golden halo.

Then, the Parker-Bowles thing happened, the tampax tapes, the bulimia expose, the James Hewitt love affair, the Dodi Fayed pics on the boat, Di in her leopard-print bathing suit talking on her cell on a speedboat in the middle of the Mediterranean in August. Would she marry him? Was she pregnant? The little princes sped around on their speedboats without a thought to the evil lurking in the outside world, the trouble brewing in Sandringham, the family summer residence, and the place where Diana grew up next door to the Royal family. Did you know she was a childhood playmate of Princes Andrew and Edward and that she had a poster of Charles hung over her bed in her dorm room?

No, you probably didn't know these things, as I do. I have read at least ten biographies of Diana and viewed hundreds of TV shows, read hundreds of newspaper and magazine articles. And then came the death day. Or night, as it was, in the middle of August in 1997 that Diana died in that car wreck in Paris. I immediately said, "This was an assassination."

"Fucking Royal Family," I thought. I can see it now. Old Phillip pulling wimpy Charles into the Royal chamber. "Off with her head now, boy. . . Stiff upper lip." The Royal Family has a history of offing their undesirables. Look at Henry the Eighth. And Diana had pushed the envelope a little too far in her war with her in-laws.

So, now comes the funeral, and I woke at 5:00 AM and watched the sad procession through the streets, saw the piles of flowers, and hated the Queen for her lack of early participation. I saw the little note left by Harry on the top of the casket that went to Althrop for burial. When I heard the Earl of Spencer's speech, I was blown away. It was so adamant and eloquent.

Now, this week, eight years later, comes Camilla back to marry Charles. And the world is accepting her. Even Harry and William are putting on the brave front. Maybe they do love her, that "Rottweiler." I don't. I am thinking of Diana and that this woman made her life miserable.

Now Diana and I have something in common. A woman comes along, takes your place at the dinner table, and you watch helplessly while life goes on. At least the English hit squad didn't off me. Thank God, I remained to find a different paradise earth.

Lightning

I am returning from a week at the beach with my friends and family. We have driven the four hours from the shores of Delaware to our home in suburban Maryland and arrived at the darkest moment of the night.

As we unload the car, a strange smell assaults our nostrils. It smells of rotten meat, but there is no clue as to where this terrible odor is emanating from. It is very late, and we are tired. I am tired from the long drive and tired of a marriage that is not working. I am exhausted. I drag the heavy suitcases to the upstairs bedroom and leave the sandy, damp clothing for its bath tomorrow. The suitcase is stuffed with memories of a week pretending to be a family. A happy family as we imagine our friends to be.

But this happy family goes to sleep with each member in their own world. The children are in their rooms, and my husband and I return to our own isolation. This is a world of deep resentment and suspicion. It smells as rancid as the odor outside our home. The putrid cloud drifts through the open windows and climbs into our white bed. The smell is between our sheets.

I turn my back to my husband and build a wall of pillows between our sweaty bodies. The sun has freshened our cheeks to a bright pink, but the soul is charred. Burnt to a crisp and black with deceit. And the odor has now invaded the lacy pillow I place over my head.

Escape. I want to run from the trapped feeling of the stulti-fied relationship. There is no way out. Nowhere to hide from the stench of rotten meat.

In the morning, I follow my nostrils to the back of the house, and there—just feet from the back door—a deer. A baby deer is rotting in the hot sun of an August morning. Struck by lightning, the doe died trying to escape the storm. Her body is rotting on the earth. There is no escape. The brown soft eyes are still open. The smell is obnoxious. I want the soft fragrance of Jergen's baby powder. I do not want to smell the rotten meat leftover from a ter-rible storm several days gone.

The trash men remove the deteriorated body of the tiny deer, and on the earth is a scorched black patch where the animal has been struck by the intense heat. The exact outline of a baby deer remains an imprint on my once green grass for weeks.

I am reminded each time I open the back door of the power of the lightning and its destruction. And of the rotten smell. It is the emblem of my life, which is torn apart by anger. Lightning struck in my yard today. Near my backdoor, up my steps, through the family room and into my bed. It struck once to kill the deer, and it will strike again, soon, to kill my marriage.

The Tipping Point

Yesterday I had lunch with an artist at the lovely community of Towles Court in downtown Sarasota. We sat on the porch of the beautiful restaurant "La Vanda." It was misting, soft foggy wisps, creating a silver pearl shell. The light was filtering in that certain way that changes the ordinary to the extraordinary. It was a rain day. Florida rain days are like northern snow days. It's a time to excuse yourself from reality and slip into a dreamlike trance. It's a chance to find a nest and cover yourself with clean white down.

I was ordering grilled shrimp on a bed of spinach with feta and black olives. Oh yes, toasted pine nuts. Lots of sautéed pine nuts. I asked my artist friend, "How do we know when enough is enough?"

"Well, let me tell you. When I was in New York working as an editor on a magazine, I walked into my office. A memo swirled by my desk, and at that moment I couldn't take it anymore. Not one minute more. I stepped into the end office where the boss worked, and I said, 'I am leaving! Not in two weeks, not in two hours, not in two minutes, but now.' I walked back to my office, packed my belongings, and strode out onto Madison Avenue." She finished her statement with a fork jabbed into her grilled Portobello mushroom.

I thought about what she said and I answered, "Every once in a while I leave a situation when I am supposed to leave. But most of the time I stay way too long. My loyalty borders on co-addiction. I like living inside of a silver shell. The tipping point will arrive soon enough, without any help from me."

Who knows when that tipping point arrives? It's when impulse and memory intersect and suddenly you are out the door. You check for your wings to make sure they are still there. You take the first step, the wings flap and you're gone. You don't know where you are going, but you are gone.

art by Jill Pankey

DINING OUT
IN SARASOTA

New Beginnings

She was a newcomer to the town of Sarasota, Florida. Only one month earlier, she had been sleeping in an awkward position in the coach of the Autotrain that took her and her new husband from Lorton, Virginia to Orlando. In Orlando, they hopped off the train and into the old Toyota, silver blue, speeding along Interstate 75 with anticipation for their new life in the Sunshine State. The sun was setting over the Gulf of Mexico when they arrived at their small, but well-loved, home.

There they were—the two palm trees, shadowed against the evening sky, just as she remembered. She could just make out the golf course in the back. They were situated on the first hole of the HERON course. The sand trap that bordered their property was already asleep. The next morning they were awake at seven, the voices of golfers calling "fore" and chatting on the first hole.

She loved her little home away from home. With two years left until she could collect her teacher's pension, she continued to travel back and forth to the high school in suburban Maryland. The school had changed from all white, middle class, to a highly integrated, multi-cultural gaggle of teenagers. The international culture of Washington, D.C. had spilled to the suburbs, and speaking to kids who spoke in as many as twenty different languages made teaching English more than difficult. She was ready to leave that job and move into the house with the two palms.

Here in Florida was a different life. . . .a new start. She knew no one. Not a single person. Not her ex-husband, or his family. Not his kids or her high school buddies. Just Hubby, and he was not a soulmate. He played golf two or three days a week, or he puttered in the yard or repaired the greasy engine on his '67 Olds.

So, she began to write. She would stare at the computer screen, blue and white, glowing in the dim light. She would stare. . . and stare at that screen. Then one day her fingers began to move, one letter at a time. Sometimes her fingers would move by themselves as if she were giving birth to her ideas, and the muscles would contract to spit out ideas she didn't know existed. Her stories would have lives of their own; they would wander up and down hills, to the heavens and to hell, only to return to the sandy shores of Siesta Key Beach.

She found her stories carrying her back and back to places she forgot she knew. Places where her mother was still alive, still beautiful, and busy meeting her friends for lunch, playing mahjongg or shopping for new clothes. Her father was alive, silver-haired and silent, turning the pages of the New York Times or The Washington Post, his glasses thick, his thoughts impenetrable. Her brother was a bother then, with big ears and clipped hair. He followed her everywhere. She had forgotten about his big ears until she began her stories, her forays into those forgotten years.

Santa Fe Dream

*H*ubby-Two and I had met at a boat party in Sarasota in July of '97 and discovered that we had a mutual love of the Southwest. I discovered that Hubby had a fantastic southwest art collection, a camera and a talent for taking fine photos. I learned that he loved to travel and was funny and creative.

By then, the separation from Hubby-Ex was in full swing; Hubby-Two helped me through the divorce, pulled me out of the deep hole that took twenty-seven years to dig. He was logical and showed me the flaws in my fake reality and denial of the truth. He exposed Hubby-Ex like an x-ray or an MRI.

Over the years, I had traveled to New Mexico for writing classes, photography classes, and for just plain fun. Sometimes I ended up in the state five times a year. I'd dreamed of having my own home, but, as building a small adobe home on the little piece of property I had bought never came to fruition, I scrapped the plans when Hubby and I married several years later.

"We'll live in Florida," he said. "It's closer to work and more practical for us." And he was right. I love my life in Sarasota. I have a little routine going. Monday is my writing class that I teach. Three days a week at the YMCA. Wednesday afternoons I discuss Carl Jung with another group of interesting folks. Thursday and Saturday are also devoted to writing. Sunday is for Hubby and me to sleep late and read the paper in bed.

So, where is the horror story? I am ashamed to admit that I am afraid to spend this summer in Santa Fe. We have finally realized our dream and purchased a small lot near the Opera. We have rented a home for July, August and September. We plan to leave the last week in June and drive to Santa Fe in the new Toyota truck Hubby bought last summer. My entire dream—but I am afraid of a nightmare.

What will I do without my routine, my familiar bed and my little life I have created here in Sarasota? What about the fountains in the pool, which start to flow at 11:00 AM? Three months seems so long, and I am scared that I will face empty days and nights. No friends or family, what will I do for the hours to fill the afternoons. How could I make this decision to go away for THREE MONTHS? I am having "buyer's remorse."

Dining Out In Sarasota

f ood is the social event for the folks of Sarasota. Many of the residents are retired, not only from "work" but also from kitchen duties. When one plans an outing, the first question is always, "Where shall we eat?"

This is a resort town. The restaurants grow—multiply like termites—go in and out of business. There is always a new place to try, a new chef to experience, or a special dish to order. There is one huge problem with dining out that is inevitable. That is the bill. Who pays is what causes many disagreements. Friends have been known to stop speaking to one another as a result of disagreements over a restaurant bill.

"Can I have a separate check?" Louis may ask.

"I need a separate check, too," says Wally. "We have an Entertainment coupon."

"Let's split the check," says another.

"Who had the wine? Who had the martini? What about the diet coke with lime?"

"What about the tip?" asks Louise.

"15%," says the man in the gray sweater at the table of fourteen people.

"No, 20%. I always tip 20%," says the other man in the red polyester golf shorts.

"What about the taxes?" asks Louise, who is wearing the sweater with the stitched pink flamingos.

And so it goes, on and on. Who pays what? What if there is a recently separated or widowed woman who is a friend of the plaid-jacket man? Does he pay for her, or is her bill divided up among everyone at the table? Or does the woman want to pay for herself?

Once or twice, some generous or drunk dinner companion will say, "Put your money away, folks. Dinner is on me!"

Or, on another occasion, we will dine at a country club that doesn't accept cash. In this case, the member will pick up the tab.

Dining out is complicated in the Sunshine State. There are the people with fixed incomes, and people who clip dining coupons. Some others are fabulously wealthy, jumping off their yacht to join a crowd of friends at Marina Jack's. And then there are the "early bird specials" that require one to eat at 5:00 PM.

"It's a great deal," Helen will say as she dresses for the theatre at 3:30 PM. "See you at Michael's on East at 5:00. Don't be late, or you'll have to pay the regular price."

The list of rules goes on and on. Food and more food. Me, I enjoy the oatmeal with brown sugar and raisins at The Serving Spoon on Bee Ridge Road. I eat alone and read the newspaper. No complications.

Is it Heaven or is it Hell?

It's December and time for winter season at the Homestead Club, a very upscale, snooty den of rich corporate executives, retired trust fund babies, and trophy wives. Here at "The Club," as it is so often called, are two 18-hole golf courses designed by Bobby Jones. At the entrance is a sprawling clubhouse with an equally impressive dress code. No jeans allowed! Denim may be worn only in your own home.

The mailboxes are painted Homestead green, and the paint is mixed at Potter's Paints. Gold decals for addresses must be purchased at Lonnie's Decal Shop on Bee Ridge Road and Beneva for six dollars. There is another $35 charge if the maintenance crew services your mailbox.

No cars can sleep in the driveway overnight. All vehicles must have their private bedroom, and some homes have four or five garages. Air-conditioned, no less.

Blooming Newman cares for landscaping, and the owners must leave the choice of plants, bushes, and flowers in Newman's hands so that the correct colors and styles of shrubs are planted annually on corners. Service workers of all sorts clog the street at the gated entrance.

"Howdy," yells the truck driver from Bob's Electric Service, "I'm here to visit Bessie Smithson. Appointment at 7:30 today." He peers at the Wackenhut security guard who proudly sports the trademark tan uniform with gold buttons and wide-brimmed hat.

The guard chastises the electrician. "Sorry, gates open for vendors at 8:00 AM. You'll have to wait in the left parking lot, over there." He points his bony finger to the crowded staging area. The parking lot of waiting landscapers, carpet cleaners, maids, TV repairmen, and house painters grows fuller by the minute. Soon the parade of mobile pet groomers, auto detailers, and private personal trainers will arrive.

Chemicals abound here at the Homestead. The tropical environment and the "deed restrictions" force the residents to use the services of Truly Nolen, the bug exterminator, and Chemlawn, the lawn poisoner. The pool needs chemicals, also. The roof and the driveway must be power washed constantly with toxic solutions to rid homes of black mold. The shrubbery, green lawns, and lush ferns that surround the homes dotting the landscape are sprayed once a week with some other poisonous residue.

Impatiens appear pink and white next to the bright red geraniums and yellow bougainvillea. Hibiscus blooms freely. The workers with their trimmers and blowers toil from dawn to dusk to keep the grounds just perfect. This is a perfect world here at the Homestead.

Thank goodness residents are locked inside the security gates, which open and close by permission only. Homeowners are confined to their spotless community along with their chemicals, home theaters, gyms, fountains, and silver Jaguars. We do our best, here at the Homestead, to make America a safer place to live.

New Year's Eve

Having just moved to our new home in Sarasota, we are still in the habit of importing our friends from Washington, DC.

We invite Pam and Tom, and we call Lyn and Chad—both couples from Maryland. We invite our closest neighbors, who have also moved here just several months earlier.

"Let's have a New Year's Eve party!" Everyone is looking forward to the event, and, in fact, two of the couples are staying at our home. All is cozy.

The women shop for the food and the men for the liquor. The bottles of vodka are freezing, the filet mignon pink, and the smell of freshly baked croissants wafts in the air.

Early in the evening, Hubby decides to fix the night-lights in our front yard. One thing leads to another, and by 8:00 PM I am asking him to stop puttering around.

"Dinner is ready, and so are we. Come in, and take a shower."

I have only been married two months, and I don't yet know how stubborn he can be. He ignores me completely and keeps digging in the dirt, in the dark, wearing a pith helmet, trying to fix those lights. I say to my hungry guests, who also don't know how eccentric Hubby can be, "Let's just eat without him. Maybe if he gets hungry he will come in."

The table is laden with the goodies, the glasses shine brightly under the lit brass chandelier; we all toast to the year 2000.

"Health happiness, and joy to all," says Peter.

"May the Lord bless us all," says Tom, who is an ordained minister.

"Where is Hubby?" I ask.

I get up from the table, and there he is with a flashlight, lost in his "broken-outdoor-lights" world. I try to appeal to his sense of decency,

"How could you ignore your guests like this? You are embarrassing me. You need to forget this project and come inside and eat dinner."

"OK, OK," He spends another hour cleaning his tools and putting them away. By now our guests are quite tipsy and having a wonderful time.

"Where is he?" they occasionally ask after another martini or another glass of white wine. Dessert is eaten, coffee is served, and my guests are beginning to sober up. No Hubby.

Eventually, Hubby wanders in, and heads for the shower. I wait for him to join the group. Just when Dick Clark begins counting down the minutes and we wait breathlessly for the ball to drop, I walk into the bedroom. There he is, sound asleep in his underwear in our king sized bed.

I explain to our guests that Hubby will not be joining us this evening. Fran and Peter are the first and only to leave. The other guests make their way to their bedrooms.

Just as the front door closes and the last light is turned off, Hubby jumps up in bed. Suddenly, he is wide-awake. It's 2:00 in the morning, and he is ready to party.

"Where is everyone"? He asks.

Pefectionist

Perfectionist is the last thing I would call myself. I overlook those little drops of water left on the stainless steel kitchen sink, a small flake of light-meat packed-in-water tuna may still be attached to the can when I toss it into the blue plastic recycle bin, and the corners of my newly made bed would never pass muster.

I don't care which way the toilet paper is put on the holder. Does the flap go over the roll or under the roll? Spices can be put on the shelf in any order; wherever it fits, fine with me. Cereal can go next to crackers in the pantry and the soups can be mixed with the canned veggies. The milk in the fridge can sit next to the orange juice. Honestly, I've never thought of arranging the items on my shelves in order of expiration date.

Lets see, what other crimes of omission do I make? I don't always shop for the best deal on foods and will pay too much for convenience and immediate satisfaction. I never used to check the price of gas and could not have told you whether the going price per gallon was $1.39 or $1.65. In fact, I bought gas from the more expensive station that was on the right side of the street on my way to work because they took credit cards . . . my ex was paying for gas, anyway.

I buy books at full price at Barnes & Noble. Sometimes I am reading a novel, a newspaper article, a magazine and e-mail all at the same time, finishing them all, but not in any special order. The books on my shelves are in no particular order, not arranged by topic, author, size, paperback or hardback.

My files are a shoebox containing the paperwork that my life generates. It took four months during my separation and divorce to realize that my account statements were not coming to my house but to my ex-husband's address. That's because I don't reconcile my checking account at the end of each month, nor do I verify my credit statement matching receipt to entry on the bill.

My closet makes the wreck of the Titanic a blip on the radar screen (did they have radar then?). Winter clothing hangs with summer, fall with spring, red clothing with black, blouses with slacks and so on. My shoes often pile wildly on the floor. I've gotten used to finding matchbooks from five years ago in a purse retrieved from the far corner of a back shelf. The plus side of this situation is that searching for something to wear is always a huge surprise. "Oh, I forgot I had that blouse or sweater or pair of new jeans," I mutter to myself. Possessions are unearthed like lost treasures.

When I pack for a trip, I take too many shampoos and double up on conditioners. The suitcase looks relatively neat on the day I leave for a trip, but two weeks later—what a mess! I never unpack and put everything neatly away the minute I arrive home. The suitcase gets tucked away on the attic shelf when I can't stand seeing the mess on the bed in the guestroom one more second. It's a good thing that I don't have many houseguests.

Sometimes I do the laundry at peak hours and have been known to waste energy as well as money by leaving on lights just "because." My hamper overflows with laundry; I am not a creature of habit, so the laundry does not get done every Saturday morning like clockwork. Half of what I own is in Florida and the other half in Maryland. What I want today is often south, and what I want tomorrow is often north.

My glove compartment has used toothpicks and tissues in it

until I clean it out every month or so. And you should see a rental car when I am finished with it. These are the imponderables about my daily life. The real question is, how do I make it through the world with these terrible habits? I have probably been ripped off by every restaurant in town as I never check the bill before signing on the dotted line.

OK... I could go on but will spare you more of the ugly details. My husband is a perfectionist, and HE clued me in on the orderliness in other people's lives. My faults exposed, I feel naked in front of strangers.

Epiphany

It's Monday night, a breezy kind of balmy night with tropical air and a red sky. My friend Peter is the president of Key Chorale, a well-known group of choral musicians here in Sarasota. Maybe it was originally started on Siesta Key, I don't know, but now it is a huge organization of singers, musicians, and sometimes dancers.

Tonight, the group is presenting the concert they plan to take to Italy this summer. It is their twenty-fourth anniversary, and the group will tour from Venice to Milan and on to Rome. It will also visit Nice and other areas of mountainous France. The magic of the music takes me away to another world. Not expecting to enjoy the religious choices, I am pleasantly surprised. The group sings incredible versions of "Danny Boy" and "Amazing Grace." Half of the chorus stands in the balcony.

The conductor, Joseph Caulkins, tells us we can enjoy music surround sound. Caulkins is a new young conductor. It is his energy and understanding of the creative spirit that brings this music alive. He talks with enthusiasm about the composer of one special piece. He gives the audience a history of this music. "Often an artist goes to his art to heal. This is a saving grace. The next piece you are about to hear is the struggle of this composer to come to terms with the death of his mother. He turned to his musical notes to heal his heart and to bring life back to his soul. The five movements represent his stages of grieving and renewal."

While the music echoes in the halls and rafters of the Church of the Palms, I close my eyes and dream of yellowing fall leaves and white-foamed thundering waves.

I think of the creative process channeling through my blood and bones. I think how lucky I am to have a creative outlet that allows me to understand my life's journey, to give me insight into my own suffering, and to struggle, limping all the way, to a healing port.

Academy Awards

Rose is in charge of the food. She has made a plate of brisket soaked in gravy and roasted salami that we slice and eat in about a second. Judy has brought deviled eggs and two bottles of champagne, which, unfortunately, we never open. Although Rose lost her husband just two months ago, she has brought the red felt carpet, the director's board and the gold Oscar made of reflective foil to hang on the door. I have provided a shiny top hat, tons of Mardi Gras necklaces, and an ice tub.

We have champagne flutes, but Hubby gets to work on his laundry and taxes, ignoring his job to operate his new 80-inch TV. Rose is sad because she misses her deceased Jan, but holds on until she falls asleep in the corner on the sofa under the plush blanket. Most leave early, after we have eaten all of the chocolate cupcakes sprinkled in gold foil and placed on the serving plate decorated with gold stars.

The setting was geared to have fun, fun, fun—to ignore the fact that this is the tenth year in a row that we have celebrated together, to forget how old Billy Crystal has gotten, to not notice that he looks like Mrs. Doubtfire's mother.

We admire the young and skinny starlets, but remember that we don't know a single name. We have seen most of the nominated movies, but, of course, we have forgotten the plots and the music.

Everyone leaves by 10:00 PM, just after the best actor and best actress awards. They had wanted to catch the best film award, but each is scared to drive home in the dark.

Family Matters

*F*eeling connected to a group larger than oneself is a safety net. Just look at Nick Wallenda at the Circus Sarasota.

Nick is a tightrope walker, and he holds Sarasota spellbound as he walks between buildings of downtown during Circus week. The headlines of the local newspaper, the Herald Tribune, shout: "See Nick Wallanda walk the walk!"

Folks get up at 5:00 AM just to gather in the shade of the Ritz Carlton. They are wearing their strongest sunglasses, the ones with the prescription, just to watch the death-defying act. The countdown arrives. The tightrope is dazzlingly empty. Suddenly, Nick arrives in his sequined suit with the fringe. He bows his acknowledgment to the audience, who hold their breath as he takes his first step. He is like a cat, making his way inch by inch on the high wire, seemingly lost in his concentration. The audience counts the tiny steps. One, two, three and so on, as he inches his way across Main Street with no net to catch him should his foot slip.

Nick's mother is a hostess at our country club. Norma is a slender fifty-one-year-old who still performs on the high-wire along with her children and her grandchildren. She often visits our table to talk about her famous son or about the book she has written on her relatives: "The Flying Wallendas."

"How does she stand it?" I think as she tells us about her grandfather who died when his trapeze proved an enemy. He fell to the ground in front of a live circus audience. How can she stand to watch her son traverse that trapeze every night in tandem with his cousins, his aunts, and his uncles?

"I give up control," she says. "I just believe that everything is fine and send out positive wishes. If he dies, he dies doing just want he wanted to do. It's in his blood."

Nick has the safety net of his family. They are bonded by fear morphed into belief and confidence. They are his foundation. Nick has yet to have a misstep.

Hurricane Wilma

I wake at 2:00 AM. I turn on the Weather Channel.

"Hello folks," says the cheery blonde with the shining white teeth and the perfect make-up. "Here are the latest forecasts from NOAA on this Category 5 Hurricane, Wilma, that is headed our way. First, let us show you what destruction this storm brought to Cancun." Now I watch the palm trees flying in the air and the poor peasants stumbling into yellow school buses with all of their possessions on their backs. The Americans who couldn't get out in time are holed up somewhere without food or water. No surprise.

There are one hundred white arrows and seven different colored lines that look like nerve ganglia. Each line represents a path that this Wilma might take. One of the paths is through Sarasota, but mostly the newscasters are reporting a more "southerly" route.

The worst part of the whole thing is the feeling of helplessness. The main road, Interstate 75, is packed, like the routes out of Houston with Hurricane Katrina. I would rather stay home with the dog and cat and the wind and the rain than feel claustrophobic in traffic.

Hotels are filled up and down the East Coast, and most flights are cancelled.

When I watched the hurricane victims of Katrina I asked, "Why the hell didn't they get out earlier?"

122

Now, I can see why—the hurricane anxiety is running rampant around Sarasota. Headlines in Newspaper: GO or STAY? Who knows? We are staying, and Hubby has me helping to saw plywood for the windows that are most vulnerable to the wind. We are bringing in all the outdoor furniture that was power washed and put out last week. This is not conducive to concentration, but I am hoping to go to It's a Grind, an Internet shop and get away from the panic for a few hours in the morning.

The rain has not come yet, but all events—like The Taste of Sarasota, Venice Fun and Sun Fest, Jazz on the Bay—forget it. All cancelled. There is no fun in Florida right now. My friend's son's wedding was cancelled today. No one could fly in, and basically, who the hell knows what is happening? Every hour the storm predictions change, but it looks like we still have a few more days to worry and get ready for the big event.

This morning Hubby has gone to volunteer at our Temple and brought his Phillips screwdriver to screw in hurricane shutters. This will keep him busy for most of the day, and then I will be forced into slave labor once again.

When he left he said, "This is good. I will be able to see if it is worth the investment for our home." These shutters are expensive and difficult to install. But, at least I won't be hauling plywood through the living room, measuring, sawing and doing Home Depot-type-projects. I am not a big fan of screwdrivers or Home Depot.

Parking Space

*L*ast Sunday morning at 9:00 AM, Hubby and I picked up Meredith and Linda, new friends here at the Homestead Country Club. The four of us were attending a memorial service for Alvin Simovitch, who had died just two days earlier. Alvin had been president of our Temple Sinai for the last few years. The congregation had anticipated his death after a long illness. There were hundreds of members and friends attending the mourners' service.

Hubby dropped us off at the front door as he parked the car. The women were dressed in black with long sleeves covering their bare shoulders. Men honored Alvin by wearing ties and jackets even though it was summer in Florida. The temperature was nearing the one hundred mark, accompanied by ninety percent humidity. By 11:00 AM, the long memorial service was over. We wiped our tears and walked to the parked car, where our name was prominently displayed on the front window. The Homestead parking pass is a coveted item when dining at the country club. Definitely not needed when parking at Temple Sinai.

I was shocked to discover that Hubby had parked in the space that had belonged to the recently deceased Alvin Simovitch. Since Alvin had been past president of the temple, everyone knew his name, and his parking space was instantly recognizable. A large sign marked the space as RESERVED FOR TEMPLE PRESIDENT.

"How could you do this?" I demanded of Hubby. "This is so inappropriate!"

"What's wrong?" answered Hubby. "He doesn't need it anymore!"

Winston at Neiman's

*a*t lunch, Lyn turns to smile at me. I am a new acquaintance. "What do you want to do after this?" she asks. While I digest my Cobb salad with Maytag Bleu cheese and she wipes the strawberry shreds from her front teeth, I answer, "Ringling Museum?"

"OK," she says, "but I have to pick up my Tod bag from Neiman's, and I have to check Louis to see if they got anything new."

We head to Neiman Marcus at the University Town Center Mall, where we meet a saleswoman, who asks, "Where is Winston?"

"Oh," answers Lyn, "It's too hot out today for his walk."

Winston is Lyn's little well-groomed terrier, who has a jeweled collar. On the average, Lyn takes Winston for a walk three times a day through the mall.

"He can even walk the escalator himself. He can find his way to Chanel dresses blindfolded."

So can Lyn. She knows every purse that costs over $2,500.

"This morning I bought this one in gray and raspberry," and she points to two Chanel bags, the price of which would feed the average family for a month.

The salesman at Louis Vuitton kisses her hand as we stroll into the pristine shop. The air is white and the scent is gardenia. "Lyn, dahling! It has been sooo long since I have seen you. You look wonderful! But you always look wonderful."

Lyn points to the driving loafers that she has in blue, black, and dark green. "They are the most comfortable shoes," she says to me, "next to my Manolos, of course. Don't you just love Jimmy Choo, too?" And she flashes her brilliant white smile as we head to the Burberry store to buy some dog clothing for Winston

Later that evening, Hubby and I meet Lyn and David for dinner. They never eat dinner at home. Every night Lyn makes reservations, and her husband meets her at 6:30 PM.

"You can set your clock by it," Lyn explains.

Splitting the $500 bill, Hubby and I are treated to rich desserts by the owner, who visits the table five or six times during our meal.

The owner coos, "Lyn, where have you been? I haven't seen you for a week." He kisses the same hand that the guy at Vuitton's kissed just hours before.

This is how Lyn and David live. When they travel, David explains, they always spend at least $800 a night for a room, and they only fly first class. Never on Southwest.

Winston stays at the doggie lodge in a luxury room. He has his own bed and a television.

David works five days a week and bills twenty-five hundred hours a year as a tax lawyer, and Lyn spends to give him a reason for working so much.

"So, how is your son Bill?" Hubby asks. Lyn's eyes well up. Tears begin to spill over her cheeks.

"He killed himself three years ago. He shot himself in the head."

David, her husband, nods his head. "We didn't have a clue. We were totally shocked when the phone call came from the police."

Meet the shopaholic who is married to the workaholic. David grabs the check. No coffee. No time to talk. No time to think. Just work, eat, and sleep. Lyn shops.

Eating Meatballs

*L*ast Saturday I woke up with Hubby and watched him leave for golf at 8:00 AM. I meant to go to the gym and exercise. I meant to go and pick up that quilt at the discount dry cleaners on Clark Road. But I downloaded a book on my Kindle and began to read. Suddenly, it was 9:30 AM. Still in my tee shirt and flannel pants, I didn't move an inch except to adjust the pillows.

"I'll get dressed," I thought. So I changed from the tee shirt and the flannels into to a sweatshirt and jeans with an elastic waist, but left the socks on. I puttered to the kitchen, my dogs following, and thought I would have just a little bite to eat before I went to the gym.

But there they were—the meatballs left from dinner last night and, oh, the shredded Parmesan cheese we bought at BJ's Wholesale Warehouse. Not the powdered kind made from processed cheese, but real cheese with flavor. I looked on the label and checked out the fat and the calories, and began to count the pile of numbers as the tablespoons grew on top of the meatballs.

I let the French bread sit alluringly on the counter, ate the meatballs and cheese, and then glanced at the clock. "One more chapter," I thought, and I went back to Blue Nights, Joan Didion's memoir about her time in the ICU waiting for her daughter, Quintana, to get well, which she never did. But at the time of the eating of the meatballs, while they were still warm and delicious, her daughter was still alive and getting married, so I was able to enjoy my Italian breakfast.

I thought, "It's 10:00, and the gym is open all day, so I'll read just a little bit more." And by 11:30 the dogs were hungry and the cat was crying, so I padded back to the kitchen for one can of chunky chicken dog food and one tiny tin of cat tuna. And soon I was rummaging for the leftover pastries from Morton's—the ones I served the Tuesday before at my friend Larry's birthday party. I had a little of the coconut cake—just one slice—and some coffee. By now it was almost noon, and I had a couple of hours left to be alone until Hubby returned from the eighteenth hole.

I loved the solitude and the quiet. But then the daughter in Didion's memoir was getting ill, and I had to spend another couple of hours reading about what happened, and soon I heard the door open, and it was 2:00 PM, and Hubby asked, "What's for lunch," and "Are there any meatballs left?" And I said "No, how about the Hebrew National salami we bought?" So we broke that out and put it on rye with deli mustard and, oh yeah, the coleslaw from Albertson's. And now it was almost 3:00 PM, and the daughter was dying, and I had to finish the chapter. And then it was 4:00 PM, and wasn't it just getting too late to go to the gym?

I had to dress for dinner, so I read Blue Nights until the daughter died, and I was just too exhausted and sad to go to the gym, and it was 5:00 and getting dark anyway.

This was my Saturday alone last week, and please don't tell anyone.

Safe

I hate to lose things. I am so lonesome for those two Cartier watches that were lost and put away somewhere "safe." But isn't "safe" an illusion? We think we are safe, but a beam can fall from the ceiling in your kitchen and land on your head. Boom! Now you have brain damage, and the world is caving in.

I often think of the guy in Tampa who looked forward to his bedtime pleasure. The sky had darkened and the linens were fresh. The pillows plumped just so. The room smelled like fresh water, and it was comfortable to sink into the safe nest. He didn't set his alarm because he had no reason to wake up. He could sleep as late as he wanted, until the sun crept under the front door and all that was invisible during the nighttime hours became visible. Then, as he put his head on the pillow, the ground began to shake. And that was it. He never saw the light of day again.

The *Tampa Herald Tribune* reported the damage. Around midnight a sinkhole opened and swallowed his house. His body was lost forever, buried under the tons of dirt. Alive! I hope he didn't wake up. I hope he didn't struggle for breath and die a suffocating claustrophobic death.

Nothing is safe, but we struggle to believe all is safe. Put in the safety deposit box. Is the bank account insured by the FDIC? Is this medical procedure safe? Is the dog food from China safe? Are the roads safe? Is stopping at a red light safe? Can I pull around the corner on that busy highway? Always judging risk and reward, the fragility of life is in our unconscious.

The watches are safe somewhere. Put in a safe place, like the man who went to sleep in his safe bedroom, never to see the light of day again.

Siesta Key Sunday Night

*D*rums drum, and the snake lady snakes, and the candles flicker in their little cocoons dug in the cool sand. One candle for each hour on the imaginary clock drawn in the crystal sand. Mothers and fathers and babies and wizened ones stare with pleasure at the fire, its sparks singing to the new moon as it rises in the colored blush of dusk.

The sounds of tambourines and clapping hands drift through the ears to the heart like well-written words. Sand chairs and blankets surround the dancers and the musicians. A few beers downed by the guy with the long gray ponytail. The smell of pot and incense sits upon the beach like another singer or dancer. No one notices . . . no one cares.

Over there on the right is the tai chi group, dressed alike tonight in red silk and golden sandals, immersed in the pleasure of removing the stagnant energy of the week past. And, over there, on the left, is the standing-on-his-head-guy. He is always here, on the beach at sunset on Sunday. He looks with pleasure at the world turned upside down. The soft sand becomes his heaven and the sparkling tide becomes his earth.

The constant chant of celebration continues many hours past sunset. Some drift away home to prepare that lesson plan for Monday's class or a late dinner for the family. Some do homework, or the white laundry with bleach, or read the book waiting on the bedside table. For a brief moment, all feels safe in this upside down world where the ocean hangs in the sky instead of the clouds and the sand stays attached to the heaven.

Armadillos and Anti-Semitism

esterday, Hubby pointed to the holes in the ground under the big rock in the front of our home. "Look, the armadillos are back," he commented. "I thought they left last year."

"No," I said. "I saw them last spring in the back yard under the palmettos. There was an entire family. The mother walked her tiny pink babies across our yard."

"But, I can't stand the armadillos!" Hubby protests. "They dig holes in our gardens and mess up the mulch."

"Nope," I said. "The armadillos are here forever. They may move next door for a while, but they come back. They tunnel underground, and, in the spring, the babies come up for air."

We have large holes everywhere now.

Yesterday our neighbor, Bill, told us he was moving from Homestead and buying a house in Avalon, another community about ten miles up Tamiami Trail. Over lunch, Bill whispered, "Yup, there are anti-Semites here. Too many."

"How do you know?' I inquired.

"At golf this morning," he explained, "Josh Golden, whispered to me that he was Jewish. Can you imagine? Do you want to stay here when someone has to whisper that he is Jewish?"

"Oh," I replied. "So you are buying a new house because Josh whispered?"

"Well, there are other instances, but . . . " and he glanced over his shoulder, "I don't want to talk about it here."

Armadillos are like anti-Semites. You can't see them; you can't get rid of them. They live in the shadows and will be in every community, everywhere. Moving to Avalon will not solve Billy's problem. He will find the armadillo holes there, also.

art by Jill Pankey

THE STARS ARE THERE

Writing is a Blessing

I was participating in a writing class sponsored by the Center for Hope a wonderful fund for cancer survivors. I happened upon their free Wednesday class because a long-time writing teacher in Sarasota invited me to join.

Let me tell you a little about the class. First, I thought, why would I want to be around cancer survivors? Who wants to think about cancer? But, it appears that a shocking cancer diagnosis is another trauma along the road—another upsetting event that lands on some but not others.

I have listened to the writers in the class, and one woman stands out in the most heart-wrenching but transformational manner. Her name is Claire, and during week number one she wrote about her family. In great detail, she described a lovely family picnic. Every perfect element was at this event. The aunts, the uncles, the cousins, the birthday cake, and the races, the mustard-laden hot dogs and the juicy cheeseburgers piled high with melted cheese, crispy lettuce, and just-ripe tomatoes. Claire described herself as carefree and hopeful, innocent and young, and, she wrote, "As I raced past the finish line of this blissful event, I came to realize that this was the last moment I would ever be happy." What happened, I wondered? She left us hanging over a ravine.

Week after week, Claire would read her pieces, reliving moments of happiness and always leaving us at the brink of disaster. Finally, last week, she pulled out a couple of type-written pages. Unfolding each sheet as if it were a petal from a fresh rose, she began to read. She described sitting in a doctor's office. She explained that her mother and father both were diagnosed with stage four cancers. Over her life, she endured these losses, and now here she was in a doctor's office waiting for the result of her own biopsy.

Death Comes When It Will

*T*here we were, Hubby and I, just zipping along, bickering as usual about the lane he had drifted into, when Betty called me on my cell. Strange. Haven't spoken to her in months. How could she possibly know that we were in our rental car headed to the Tampa airport, not to return to Florida until fall?

That's when I heard this awful news.

Alan. It's about Alan. Alan is married to my wonderful friend, Donna. She is the kind of friend that gave me poems for my birthday and gifts when I came home from a hospital stay. She picked me up on a drizzling day in January and insisted on paying the bill at a cozy French restaurant. After the dripping cheese baked on the onion soup, she told me of her plans to travel. Alan was renting a yacht to take her family and his family, children and grandchildren, on a cruise to Alaska for ten days. He planned on flying all of them to Vancouver on a private jet. They were staying at the Fairmont, Canada's finest, and Donna was thrilled. Her wonderful generous husband.

Betty was dreary. "I thought you might not have heard." My hairdresser is Donna's hairdresser. I gave her the number many years ago, and as I was sitting in the chair with a wet black towel draped around my neck and he was combing my hair before the trim—just the ends—the hairdresser explained that Alan had been in Sarasota Memorial Hospital in the trauma unit since Monday morning.

Alan was the picture of a happy and healthy septuagenarian. He rode his bike on a daily basis, he and Donna commenting on the swaying palms, the baby blue herons, and the breezes sifting through their hair. They rode side by side, not one in front of the other. They're a team, joined by the love of travel, ballet, and life.

"He was out riding his bike," Betty said. "The new one that they just purchased, and a beauty, really. Then he fell. It was the perfect storm. He hit his hip; but worse, he hit his head. Brain trauma. He was unconscious and rushed to the hospital. The ENT could not revive him, and neither could the emergency docs. He is resting peacefully and not in any pain. Unfortunately there has been even more damage to the brain overnight. . . there is no hope for his brain at this point. Alan has a living will and has communicated his wishes. The family plans to honor that."

Life. So tenuous. Scary and sad. Donna's plans for Shakespeare in the Park, the week in New York at the ballet, and the month of August visiting castles in Ireland—now just a whiff of past re-membrances. Death, it comes when it will, engages each of us in its life-ending dance. Perhaps we ascend somewhere in the light, where hope is soft and kind. Goodbye, Alan Clare. Enjoy.

Aunt Ann

"I don't mind it," my Aunt Ann told me as Jack, her boyfriend with advanced Alzheimer's sat in the living room chair and stared out of the French doors that lead to the patio. Ann just turned eighty-five years.

Jack was vital five years ago. He played Championship Bridge in the retirement community of Leisure World. In fact, it was Jack who organized the sets and the evening, Jack who kept track of the scores and ran the championship matches. And it was Jack who sang love songs to my Aunt Ann every birthday, Thanksgiving, Memorial Day and Fourth of July. Jack loved to sing. He loved to buy jewelry, leather and fur coats, and write love notes.

Sometime about five years ago, his mind began to slip. His eyes became empty, and his voice a monotone. Sometimes he sang, but Happy Birthday would be sung on Passover and Merry Christmas carols would be sung on Yom Kippur. No matter, Ann loved him and his company.

During the past two years, Ann's back collapsed. She now sits in a wheelchair and has a private nurse. Jack would arrive at her apartment every day at 8:00 AM and take a seat in the living room, the same seat that faced the French doors, and he would sit all day. Together, they would watch old movies, talk, and often would eat an early Chinese dinner or lunch at Nancy's sandwich shop around the corner. The nurse would walk them both to the car, open the doors, place the clumsy walker in the back seat and off they would go. Both enjoyed their arrangement.

This weekend I was in Washington, D.C., and I called my Aunt Ann. "How is Jack?" I asked. She began to weep. Helpless and inconsolable she explained, "Jack's daughter didn't like me. It's not all her fault. She heard me call Jack an idiot when he wouldn't leave me alone to go to the bathroom. She heard me yell at him to shut up. But, sometimes I would get frustrated. I still loved him."

The daughter heard one too many things one too many times, and yesterday she sent an ambulance and had Jack shipped to an Alzheimer's ward an hour away from here. "I am so lonely," Ann cries, "So lonely."

She continues, "My nurse drives me to see him. Yesterday, the nurse walked into Jack's room, and another woman—she is ninety-two—was in his bed. I yelled for her to get out. I don't think Jack realized it wasn't me. I am so unhappy and helpless to change the situation. Jack's daughter is glad to get me out of their life, and plus, she and her brother will make a lot of money when they sell his two-bedroom apartment."

I live in Florida, and I see the treatment of the aged. Powerless, dependent, often handicapped, they use the gym treadmill with an oxygen tank hooked onto the side. The nurses bring them to the gym. Dinner is served at 5:00 PM, and often they are drugged or asleep in the lobbies of the Glenridge or Village Walk. The women have their silver locks curled with sulpher smelling permanent wave solution, and they have a standing manicure once a week at Natalie's salon. Buses move the old folks from the drugstore to the museum.

Getting old means losing responsibility for oneself and depending on the "kindness of strangers," to use the words of Tennessee Williams. I am turning sixty next year. I can still drive, travel, smell the honeysuckle and give my dog a bath. I can carry money in my purse and go to Starbucks for a foamy latte while I read the latest novel in the cafe.

Meanwhile, Ann is alone with her stiff back, driving an hour to see Jack, who doesn't know she is there. Her life is desperate and lonely.

I want to dance in the Santa Fe Plaza this summer, touch the smooth silver of the jewelry that sits on the blankets under the portal during the day. I want to smell the pinion and eat black beans and rice. Maybe even the meat loaf at the Zia Diner. I want to take pictures and use a new digital camera. I want to use my energy and enjoy the blue skies. I want to ride a horse and dance at El Farol's. My days to live like Aunt Ann are looming on the horizon.

Scary, isn't it?

Never Let Go

$\mathcal{A}$ man and a woman. Married for over fifty years. They both are brilliant and successful. Well educated and sophisticated. He got sick. Prostate cancer at the age of sixty-seven. Too young. Far too young.

He was given nine months. It has been three years now, and they both are locked into some crazy kind of dance that is dark, so dark I can hardly talk about it. He has suffered more pain than I want to imagine. First it was a castration. Then radiation. Then chemotherapy. Then more radiation and more chemotherapy. Then more drugs, and years went by with more surgeries on the bones and who knows where else. He doesn't want to die. She doesn't want him to die. Now all of the options have run out, and nothing is working except his fingers on the keyboard of research sites. He has gone to New York and Miami and Boston. He has gone to Tampa and Chicago and California. He has applied for every study known to man to stop the progress of his cancer and to relieve the pain.

During the most recent stay in the hospital, the social worker came into the room. She said to him, "It's time for you to think of end of life options. Hospice can come anytime." He doesn't want to die. She doesn't want him to die. So he chose another round of radiation and chemotherapy to prolong life. But can't leave the house very much. And he is white. White like a glass of milk. She is depressed. Tired. Exhausted. She doesn't want him to die. He doesn't want to die. One more month. One more week.

Now he has found a new study, but he can't be in it for six weeks. He has to hang in there for six more weeks. He has bought a helium gas machine. He has made a mask. He went to a website from the Hemlock Society. "Look at it," she said to me. "You'll see".

I googled the "no exit bag." Ten minutes under this suffocation bag and then what? A painless non-detectable way to die?

The helium tank sits in his garage. He doesn't want to die. She doesn't want him to die. Like a guillotine, the helium machine waits by the door for his just right moment.

He has asked his kids if they want to be there. He moans most of the day. The pain for both of them is unbearable. This is a dark place. A very dark place.

And yesterday, on a bright a sunny morning, I was in Publix. I walked by the balloon section. The helium tank was there, dressed in a blue and white striped festive wrap. Pink balloons stretched from one corner to another. "But you can't fool me with your cheerfulness," I thought. "I know about you, you black and dark helium. Your lethal dose lurks for him to inhale for just ten minutes." He doesn't want to die. She doesn't want him to die. Today, he hangs in by a tether like the pink balloons attached to the helium tank, floating above, whispering. Watching. Waiting.

One Life To Live

Irma was such a "balabusta," and her husband, the doctor, a "mensch." She was a great housekeeper, mother, wife, and friend. Her husband, David, the podiatrist, was so generous and kind. Everyone I knew with a bunion, hangnail, blister or broken toe went to the office, which was conveniently located on a major thoroughfare; not too much traffic and lots of parking.

Irma, who also served as the receptionist, along with the other jobs mentioned earlier, would fit anyone into the schedule. Anyone, anytime. House visits were not unheard of. David went to high school with me, so I knew him before he married Irma, before his daughters Sherry, Barbara, Lisa and son, Scott, were born.

A visit to the foot doctor's office was special. Irma loved to bake and feed people her homemade cookies and cakes. So, while I would wait for my latest treatment, Irma and I would have a cup of hot coffee, brewed fresh, several cookies, and share the intimacies of old friends. But, mostly she talked about her kids. Her life was about her family, their accomplishments, and how beautiful her oldest daughter was becoming.

"I'll have to be kicking them away from the front door soon," she would joke.

I would see the kids often at the pool, and my kids would intertwine with hers and hundreds of others for hours on hot summer afternoons. The kids would disappear, and Irma and I would chat. She loved diamonds and would proudly display her gems, which Dr. David would bestow upon her with great frequency. After all, she was his business partner, his wife, his housekeeper, and the mother of his children. He was kind and generous. He said, "Thank you" often.

The last time I saw Irma was on television on the six o'clock news. She was throwing dirt on the graves of David, Sherry, Barbara and Lisa. With the exception of Scott, her entire family had been murdered by a workman who was left to paint the house the weekend Irma went to Ocean City to visit her son for the weekend.

She looked at the workman eyeing her daughter and warned him, "Keep away from my daughter." Then she sped off in her new Mercedes.

The phone call came in the middle of the night to the beach apartment in Ocean City. The police told her there had been an accident, and that they would come and pick her up and bring her home. The wails of despair could be heard from the beach to her home four hours away.

It had happened like this: As soon as Irma drove away, her fifteen-year-old daughter came home from swim practice. The painter followed Barbara into the house, raped her, then killed her and stuffed the body in the bedroom closet. Next, Sherry returned from her job as a shoe salesgirl at Nordstrom. He stabbed her and left her body to bleed on the kitchen floor. Finally, Lisa walked in, and she was strangled and choked to death. When Dr. David returned from the office, he came in through the garage, and the murderer was waiting for him with a hammer. He split his head open.

Then the painter called 911, and when the police arrived, the carnage was in plain view. The confessed murderer led them to the bodies of each family member and to the body of his boss, the master painter. He too was dead. He had walked in on the rape of the youngest daughter. The master painter died only two days before his young wife gave birth to their first daughter.

So, there on the evening news were Irma and Scott, burying their entire family, and the chances of something like this happening to me or you are the same as the chances were for Irma.

Many years have passed since that horrible weekend, and Irma is now remarried and living in Florida. Scott is out of college, building another life.

We all have just one. . . life, that is. But today, on this sweltering summer afternoon, as I drove past Irma and David's old doctor's office, I read the new name of an unknown podiatrist on the mailbox. I remembered Irma's chocolate chip and oatmeal raisin cookies, her diamonds and, most of all, the life that Irma used to have.

This is Karen, writing in Maryland, and this is a true story.

Perfect Nail

*L*iving in Florida is an endless summer. At age fifty-one or fifty-three or fifty-five, I am younger than most. I am the baby on the block. The young kid. Time seems endless. It will be forever until I will be using that walker to sit in a booth at Mel's Diner ordering the early bird special and pointing with bent fingers at the menu while the waitress tries to decipher my order.

"I'll have the scrambled eggs and toast with butter," I'll say as the waitress leans close to my ear under the blue curls, which were done at Natalie's Beauty salon this morning. My nails will be perfect. Always perfect. Every two weeks I will have a standing appointment with Lucy, who will put acrylic nails on my crooked fingers. I will stare at the nails, turn them over on the table, and check the corners and edges.

"Thanks, Lucy. Good color." It will be an iridescent peach to match the blush I have applied too heavily on my thin and drooping cheeks. The makeup applied to my face stops at the chin, and my neck is a different color. My eyeliner is askew, and my eyes dip downwards at the corners. The hands are thin with veins popping out as if groundhogs built burrows under the translucent skin. Spots cover the hands in various shades of chocolate and tan. All colors and sizes of spots form a map for the groundhogs living beneath the surface.

But the nails look perfect.

It is the perfect nail that points to the item on the menu at the diner; the perfect nail that points to the iced tea with endless refills; the perfect nail that reaches for the Sweet and Low to pour onto the icy drink that sits taller than I do.

My shoulders are hunched, and my neck hangs far forward to edge closer to the Formica table at Mel's.

It will be forever until I am sitting across from some young fifty-year-old who watches me with baited breath, hoping that the waitress brings my soft eggs before I draw my last breath.

In Florida, the waitress is the midwife to death. Church is from 4:00 to 5:30 when all dinners are half price or two-for-one if a partner is still alive.

The waitress explains, "Oh gosh, honey, that woman who sat next to you last week? She died yesterday."

And today, in her place, there is a man with hunched shoulders and a long nose, who points to the menu and orders eggs, fried not scrambled, with pancakes, not toast.

Third Act

ose is in Naples, Florida this weekend with her third soul mate. Her husband number one was a saint. He did drink a little too much, and he did love those nude hot tub parties in the '70s and '80s. He was the only man she had ever slept with because Rose married when she was nineteen, lived in the suburbs of Indianapolis, and raised three kids. She had a beautiful life and a beautiful home. She was best friends with her sister-in-law and had hundreds of country club friends. Rose was a model, and she posed for catalogs that showed the stylish, Midwestern happy and chic homemaker. All was great until Leonard died of leukemia at fifty-eight.

About four months later, a friend called her. "Rose, I want to fix you up with a wonderful man. He remembers you from Indiana University. He was in a fraternity and he saw you at a sorority dance."

"That was thirty-two years ago," Rose said. But the new man came over, and it was just before Thanksgiving, and she fell madly and deeply in love on the spot. Rose was married about seven years later on the beach in La Jolla. Their life was charmed. He loved her and wanted to take her away from the entire more traditional country club/martini drinking life. So they moved to Sarasota, Florida and began a new and exiting journey together.

About five years later, he succumbed to kidney failure and was on dialysis for eight years until he died.

"It's over for me," said Rose. "My life is dinners with the widows."

Then she broke her femur bone and ended up in rehab in a wheelchair. Finally, one day she said, "Get me out of here, or I will die a very lonely woman." She pushed and pushed, and suddenly she could walk without a cane, and then she dyed her hair, bought new bras, and a red lipstick.

She said, "I don't need Match.com. Someone will fix me up."

She put that wish out into the universe. Her dream arrived in the form of a new man. He is just the right age, just the right size, and just the right religion. He is a Republican from the Midwest, and he, too, remembered her from college. He was a fraternity brother of her second husband.

It seems that lightning has struck three times for Rose. She is on a four-day jaunt with her new man to Naples, Florida. And did I mention he owns a travel agency? Soon the third act will be a cruise around the world. Rose has found the eighteen-year-old self of her sophomore year. . . the self that she had thought was lost forever. Oh, did I mention he brought roses on the first date; tulips with a Tiffany necklace on the second date?

Small Wonders

Sandhill cranes stroll the golf course,
Traverse the sandy streets
With a power unknown to me.
Trucks and SUVs stand at attention
When this trio of elegant birds
Take their daily stroll.

Red heads of three birds,
Six strong spindly legs.
Each bird stands in the middle of the road
Every day like clockwork.

Wind does not stop them, and rain doesn't faze them,
They gaze at the headlights of the waiting cars.
Five minutes to reach the other side of the road.
No horns honk, no one yells, "Get outta the way!"

Even the busy landscapers stare in awe
At the majesty and the confidence
Of these three sandhill cranes.
It is a religious epiphany,
The steadfastness of these birds.

One gazes at these small wonders
Retracing their steps on a daily basis,
Amazed at the power of the universe.
No past, no future, just the now
And the tiny steps of the sandhill cranes
Crossing the street at 10:10 AM.

The Stars are There
Even in Full Sun

*W*hat you want is unconscious. You think you are in control, making choices based on what is obvious. You make choices because of money or health or circumstance. It's planned, this life of yours. Oh, you moved to Florida because your friend was there. But then, a few years later, you are painting watercolors with a talent you never knew you possessed. You are slicing avocadoes on a red plate.

You are performing at a variety of venues, reading stories to strangers that you now know but never knew before. You are president of the sisterhood, treasurer of this organization, on the board of that one. You are traveling to wondrous places that were just pictures in your dreams years earlier. The circumstance that brings you here now, in this space, under this sun, under this full moon, is not your choice. It is the choice of the unconscious. Somewhere in that intuitive nature, you stopped to throw away years of photos and a poem drops from the pages.

You plan a dinner with friends, and your husband is ill, or you fall and break your nose. But, when you broke your nose, you found a doctor that saw a growth on your eye, which he removed, and aren't you lucky it's only stage one cancer, and you are cured? But some time later, just when that eye is better, someone you know dies in a car crash while visiting his children. The fortune is left to the kids, who build a highway with the name of the father. Then, of all things, the son dies on that road that is named after the father. You think you know where you are going, but you are led, and sometimes you see or hear the signs. The reason might not be revealed to you, but the words are there if you just listen.

A Different Vibe

Stillness in Sarasota comes in the summer. It's the kind of place where alligators crawl across your front yard and sleep in the street. The neighbors call the security guards, who eventually get around to calling animal control, who eventually get around to the alligator problem, but by then the alligator has finished his afternoon snooze and is back in the cool stillness of the nearby water.

The egrets used to roost here in the spring and summer until Paige, an angry neighbor, got tired of it. She went out to the bird sanctuary where the white egrets congregated. She aimed her shotgun, and soon there was a fire, and now the birds don't roost on her lanai. Florida is like that. . . a slow moving spirit like molasses. It seeps into your pores and makes you wait for the inevitable, perhaps on the golf course or at the bridge table.

Santa Fe, now that's a very different vibe. The town is a puzzle, but the pieces don't fit just right. Once in a while the picture becomes clear, and the steps are in front of you, but mostly Santa Fe is a mystery. The gods are kind; then they turn on you as fast as the lightning that streaks through the mountains in the late afternoons. The sky darkens; the shadows become gold, and the theatre begins. Even the opera uses the red mountains as its backdrop. Santa Fe is a mystery to me, but I am headed that way... blindfolded.

Do It Now

o bake a coconut cake with fluffy frosting, or make chocolate chip cookies and eat every one of them. Devour cherry dots and Raisinets, malted milk balls, and buttered popcorn. Drink sugary Coke with crushed ice and spoon Rocky Road ice cream into your mouth. Pile whipped cream into a huge frosted glass and dive into the pile. . . Do it now. Go to India and to the Orient.

Go find the most beautiful beach in the world. Lie on the Crescent Beach on Siesta Key. Find the most turquoise of waters. Yes, go to Greece and float from boat to boat, island to island. Lie nude in the sun. Kiss the white walls of Mykonos.

Climb the steps to the lookout points in Rocky Mountain National Park. Find the Hoh Rain Forest. Ride your bike in Stanley Park. Walk to City Lights Bookstore from the most expensive, glamorous, luxurious hotel in San Francisco.

Buy a Sub-Zero instead of the Kenmore. Change your dust ruffle and your mattress cover. Paint the walls orange, and turn the mirror on its side. Buy naked hula dancer lamps for the night table. Hang a paper-mache heart on the wall above your head. Have Gerbera daises in orange, yellow, and red in a basket on your dresser.

Do all of this right now. This very minute. Don't wait. You will be as thin as a skeleton soon enough. You might as well have mint chocolate chip Wednesdays and hot fudge Sundays.

CPSIA information can be obtained
at www.ICGtesting.com
Printed in the USA
FFHW021600310519
52749084-58278FF

9 781614 935902